031324
128
9781960604200 (GG Coil Bound Book)
9781944607852 (KDP Perfect Bound Book)
97819446078521 (VS PDF Book)
9781944607869 (eBook)

Notice: Although IconLogic makes every effort to ensure the accuracy and quality of these materials, all material is provided without any warranty.

Copyright: 2024 by IconLogic, Inc. This document, or any part thereof, may not be reproduced or transmitted in any form or by any means, electronic or mechanical, including photocopying, recording, storage in an information retrieval system, or otherwise, without the prior written permission of IconLogic.

Trademarks: IconLogic, Inc., and the IconLogic logo are registered trademarks of IconLogic. All companies and product names are trademarks or registered trademarks of their respective companies. They are used in this book in an editorial fashion only. No use of any trade name is intended to convey endorsement or other affiliation with IconLogic books.

CenarioVR: The Essentials
(Second Edition)

Kevin Siegel

"Skills and Drills" Learning

Contents

CenarioVR: The Essentials (Second Edition)

About This Book
- The Author vi
- IconLogic vi
- Book Conventions vii
- Confidence Checks vii
- Hardware and Software Requirements viii
- CenarioVR Scenarios and Asset Files viii
- How Software Updates Affect This Book ix
- Contacting IconLogic ix

Preface
- Getting Started with Virtual Reality Training 2
- VR Cameras 3
- Filming in 360 4
- The Roller-Coaster Effect vs. Teleporting 5
- Camera Positioning 5
- Stitching 6

Module 1: Scenarios and Scenes
- The CenarioVR Interface 8
  - Guided Activity 1: Import a Project into CenarioVR 8
  - Guided Activity 2: Explore the CenarioVR Interface 10
    - Preview Confidence Check 12
- New Projects 13
  - Guided Activity 3: Create a New Scenario and Add Scenes 13
  - Guided Activity 4: Manage Scenarios and Scenes 16
    - New Scenarios and Scenes Confidence Check 19

Module 2: Hotspots, Info Cards, and Images
- Hotspots 22
  - Guided Activity 5: Import a Project 22
  - Guided Activity 6: Add a Hotspot 23
  - Guided Activity 7: Add a Hotspot Action 25
- Info Cards 27
  - Guided Activity 8: Add an Info Card 27
- Images 29
  - Guided Activity 9: Add an Image 29
- Initial Views 30
  - Guided Activity 10: Set the Initial View 30
- Image and Transparent Hotspots 31
  - Guided Activity 11: Add an Image Hotspot 31
  - Guided Activity 12: Edit a Hotspot Action 33
  - Guided Activity 13: Add a Transparent Hotspot 34
    - Hotspots Confidence Check 35

Module 3: Audio, Groups, and Conditional Actions
- Audio 40
  - Guided Activity 14: Add Audio to a Scene 40
    - Audio Confidence Check 42
  - Guided Activity 15: Attach Audio to an Object 43
  - Guided Activity 16: Control Object Visibility 46
    - Object Visibility Confidence Check 48
- Grouping 50
  - Guided Activity 17: Add an Info Card and Image Hotspots 50
  - Guided Activity 18: Group Objects 53

Contents

Conditional Actions 55
  Guided Activity 19: Create IF/AND Conditions 55
  Guided Activity 20: Create IF/OR Conditions 58
    Conditional Actions Confidence Check 59

Module 4: Layers, Drag and Drop, and Timed Events
Layers 64
  Guided Activity 21: Create a Layer 64
Drag and Drop 68
  Guided Activity 22: Make an Object a Drop Spot 68
  Guided Activity 23: Make an Object a Drag Item 69
    Drag and Drop Confidence Check 70
  Guided Activity 24: Add a "Reset" Action 72
Timed Events 74
  Guided Activity 25: Insert an Action Object 74
  Guided Activity 26: Add Timed Events 75
    Timed Actions Confidence Check 77
Motion Paths 78
  Guided Activity 27: Create and Edit a Motion Path 78

Module 5: Quizzes and Variables
Quizzes 82
  Guided Activity 28: Add a Quiz Question 82
  Guided Activity 29: Set Up Quiz Question Feedback 87
    Quiz Question Confidence Check 89
Variables 92
  Guided Activity 30: Use a Variable to Display Quiz Results 92
    Conditional Actions Confidence Check 95
  Guided Activity 31: Create Custom Variables 97
  Guided Activity 32: Add a "Modify Variable" Action 98
    Custom Variables Confidence Check 100

Module 6: Publishing
Scenario Settings 104
  Guided Activity 33: Edit Scenario Settings 104
Publishing 107
  Guided Activity 34: Publish as HTML5 108
SCORM 110
  Guided Activity 35: Publish as SCORM 110
    Publishing Confidence Check 111

© 2024, IconLogic. All Rights Reserved.

Notes

"Skills and Drills" Learning

About This Book

This Section Contains Information About:

- The Author, page vi
- IconLogic, page vi
- Book Conventions, page vii
- Confidence Checks, page vii
- Hardware and Software Requirements, page viii
- CenarioVR Scenarios and Asset Files, page viii
- How Software Updates Affect This Book, page ix
- Contacting IconLogic, page ix

The Author

Kevin Siegel is the founder and president of IconLogic, Inc. He has written hundreds of step-by-step computer training books on applications such as *Adobe Captivate, TechSmith Camtasia, Articulate Storyline, Articulate Rise, iSpring Suite, Adobe RoboHelp, Adobe Presenter, Adobe Technical Communication Suite, Adobe Dreamweaver, Adobe InDesign, Microsoft PowerPoint, QuarkXPress,* and *PageMaker.*

Kevin spent five years in the U.S. Coast Guard as an award-winning photojournalist and has three decades' experience as a print publisher, technical writer, instructional designer, and eLearning developer. He is a certified technical trainer, a veteran classroom instructor, and a frequent speaker at trade shows and conventions. Kevin holds multiple certifications from Adobe and CompTIA. He is also a Certified Online Training Professional (COTP) with the International Council for Certified Online Training Professionals (ICCOTP). You can reach Kevin at **ksiegel@iconlogic.com**.

IconLogic

Founded in 1992, IconLogic is a training, development, and publishing company offering services to clients across the globe.

As a **training** company, IconLogic has directly trained tens of thousands of professionals both on-site and online on dozens of applications. Our training clients include large and small organizations such as Adobe Systems, Inc., Urogen, Agilent, Sanofi Pasteur, Kelsey Seybold, FAA, Office Pro, Adventist Health Systems, AGA, AAA, Wells Fargo, VA.gov, American Express, Lockheed Martin, General Mills, Grange Insurance, Electric Boat, Michigan.gov, Freddie Mac, Fannie Mae, ADP, ADT, Federal Reserve Bank of Richmond, Walmart, Kroger, Duke Energy, USCG, USMC, Canadian Blood, PSA, Department of Homeland Security, and the Department of Defense.

As a **development** company, IconLogic has produced eLearning and technical documentation for Duke Energy, World Bank, Heineken, EverFi, Bank of America, Fresenius Kabi, Wells Fargo, Federal Express, Fannie Mae, American Express, Microsoft, Department of For-Hire Vehicles, DC Child and Family Services, DCORM, Canadian Blood, Cancer.org, MLB, Archrock, NEEF, CHUBB, Canadian Natural Resources, and Hagerty Insurance.

As a **publishing** company, IconLogic has published hundreds of critically acclaimed books and created technical documents for both print and digital publication. Some of our most popular titles over the years include books on HTML, Dreamweaver, QuarkXPress, PageMaker, InDesign, Word, Excel, Access, Publisher, RoboHelp, RoboDemo, iSpring, Presenter, Storyline, Captivate, and PowerPoint for eLearning.

You can learn more about IconLogic's varied services at **www.iconlogic.com**.

Book Conventions

In our experience, people learn best by doing, not just by watching or listening. With this concept in mind, instructors and authors with years of experience training adult learners have created IconLogic books. IconLogic books typically contain a minimal amount of text and are loaded with hands-on activities, screen captures, and confidence checks to reinforce newly acquired skills. This book is divided into modules. Because each module builds on lessons taught in a previous module, it is recommended that you complete each module in succession.

Lesson Key

Instructions for you to follow look like this:

☐ choose **File > Open**

If you are expected to type anything or if something is important, it is set in bold type like this:

☐ type **9** into the text field

If you are expected to press a key on your keyboard, the instruction looks like this:

☐ press [**shift**]

Confidence Checks

As you work through this book, you will come across the Confidence Check image at the right. Throughout each module, you are guided through hands-on, step-by-step activities. To help ensure that you are grasping the content, Confidence Checks encourage you to complete a process or steps on your own—without step-by-step guidance. Because some of the book's activities build on completed Confidence Checks, you should complete each of the activities and Confidence Checks in order.

CenarioVR: The Essentials (Second Edition)

Hardware and Software Requirements

To complete the lessons presented in this book, you will need a modern computer (laptop or desktop) and a license to CenarioVR. While a license to CenarioVR is not included with this book, ELB Learning (the eLearning Brothers) offers a free CenarioVR trial available through the following website: **https://hub.elblearning.com/cenariovr-trial**.

> **Note:** The trial version of CenarioVR has some restrictions. For instance, you can only have a few scenarios in your account at any one time. Each scenario is limited to five scenes. And you cannot export scenarios nor publish them.

You will need to download this book's **project assets** (data files) that have been created specifically to support this book. (See the "CenarioVR Scenarios and Asset Files" section below.)

Also, you will be working with audio during some of the activities. You will either need a headset or a microphone and speakers.

CenarioVR Scenarios and Asset Files

You are likely anxious to dive into CenarioVR and begin working through this book. All that you need initially to create virtual reality training on your own is CenarioVR, this book, and a little imagination. However, you will quickly realize that you also need 360-degree images, standard images, audio files, and some CenarioVR projects to play with.

If you have not used CenarioVR, and this book assumes that you have not, I do not believe that you should not have to learn how to use CenarioVR on the fly as you create your own projects. Learning by discovery is not necessarily a bad thing, but it will take, and possibly waste, a lot of time. I have a better idea. You provide the computer and CenarioVR, and I will provide you with all of the project files and supporting assets that you need to learn CenarioVR, such as images and audio files.

During the following activity, you will download some assets—data files—from the IconLogic website.

Download the Book's Data Files/Project Assets

1. Download the student data files necessary to complete the lessons in this book.

   ☐ start a web browser and visit the following web address:
   https://www.iconlogic.com/data

   ☐ select your platform (CenarioVR works on both the Windows and Mac operating systems)

   ☐ click the link for **CenarioVR: The Essentials**

   CenarioVR ⌃
   • CenarioVR: The Essentials

   CenarioVR: The Essentials

2. If prompted, save the file to your computer. Make note of the location of the file download for step 4 below.

   Note: Depending upon your platform and browser, the download may begin automatically and the zipped file downloaded to your Downloads folder.

3. After the file fully downloads, close your web browser.

4. Extract the data files.

    ❑ find the **CVRData.zip** file you just downloaded to your computer

    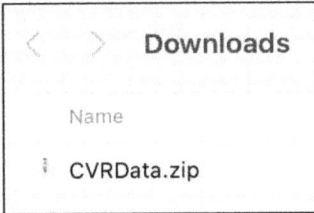

    ❑ **PC users**: right-click the downloaded file and unzip/extract it to your desktop (or other preferred location); **Mac users**: double-click the zipped file to extract it, then move the CVRData folder to your desktop

    There should be an unzipped **CVRData** folder on your computer. As you move through the lessons in this book, you will be working with these files.

    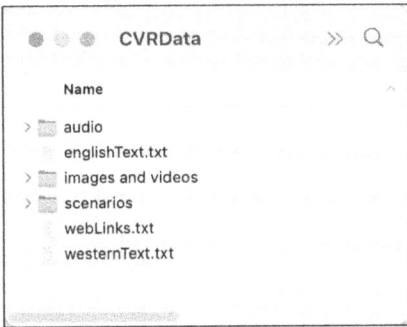

How Software Updates Affect This Book

I expect CenarioVR to get updated from time to time as new features are added. Software updates can result in a misalignment of the activities in this book and what you see while using the tool. If something on your screen does not match what I show in this book, please email me at **ksiegel@iconlogic.com** and let me know the issue. If necessary, I will update this book and/or the book's assets.

Contacting IconLogic

Web: www.iconlogic.com
Email Kevin: ksiegel@iconlogic.com
Phone: 410.956.4949, ext 711

Notes

iCONLOGiC
"Skills and Drills" Learning

Rank Your Skills

Before starting this book, complete the skills assessment on the next page.

Skills Assessment

How This Assessment Works

Ten learning objectives for *CenarioVR: The Essentials (Second Edition)* are listed below. **Before starting the book**, review each objective and rank your skills using the scale next to each objective. A rank of ① means **No Confidence** in the skill. A rank of ⑤ means **Total Confidence**. After you've completed this assessment, work through the entire book. **After finishing the book**, review each objective and rank your skills now that you've completed the book. Most people see dramatic improvements in the second assessment after completing the lessons in this book.

Before-Class Skills Assessment

1. I can add scenes to a scenario. ① ② ③ ④ ⑤
2. I can add hotspots to a scene. ① ② ③ ④ ⑤
3. I can create a motion path. ① ② ③ ④ ⑤
4. I can publish as HTML5. ① ② ③ ④ ⑤
5. I can publish a SCORM-compliant package. ① ② ③ ④ ⑤
6. I can create a drag and drop interaction. ① ② ③ ④ ⑤
7. I can create a quiz. ① ② ③ ④ ⑤
8. I can create a conditional action. ① ② ③ ④ ⑤
9. I can create a layer. ① ② ③ ④ ⑤
10. I can use an action to control audio. ① ② ③ ④ ⑤

After-Class Skills Assessment

1. I can add scenes to a scenario. ① ② ③ ④ ⑤
2. I can add hotspots to a scene. ① ② ③ ④ ⑤
3. I can create a motion path. ① ② ③ ④ ⑤
4. I can publish as HTML5. ① ② ③ ④ ⑤
5. I can publish a SCORM-compliant package. ① ② ③ ④ ⑤
6. I can create a drag and drop interaction. ① ② ③ ④ ⑤
7. I can create a quiz. ① ② ③ ④ ⑤
8. I can create a conditional action. ① ② ③ ④ ⑤
9. I can create a layer. ① ② ③ ④ ⑤
10. I can use an action to control audio. ① ② ③ ④ ⑤

IconLogic, Inc.
"Skills and Drills" Learning
www.iconlogic.com

"Skills and Drills" Learning

Preface

In This Module You Will Learn About:

- Getting Started with Virtual Reality Training, page 2
- VR Cameras, page 3
- The Roller-Coaster Effect vs. Teleporting, page 5
- Camera Positioning, page 5
- Stitching, page 6

Getting Started with Virtual Reality Training

Many people think that creating virtual reality (VR) training is expensive, time-consuming, and technically challenging. In reality, creating VR has never been easier and less expensive than today. To create a VR course, all that you need is solid instructional design, VR images or videos, voiceover audio files, and a VR development tool.

CenarioVR serves the role of VR development tool. And you'll learn how to use CenarioVR to create VR training using provided assets as you work through the activities in this book. I'll be providing all of the VR images, audio files, and other assets so you can focus entirely on using the CenarioVR software.

Once you have completed the lessons in this book, it is not a stretch of the imagination to assume that you will want to create your own VR projects. At that point, you are going to find yourself in need of something that can capture the VR pictures and/or videos.

According to **John Blackmon**, ELB Learning CTO and creator of CenarioVR, VR assets are equirectangular images and videos. The word equirectangular sounds strange, but you've likely come across equirectangular shapes before. For example, a flat map of the mostly-round Earth is equirectangular. The map resolves into a single point at the top and bottom of the globe.

John said that "VR images are, in reality, just simple JPEG files and VR videos are MP4s. Both are common file formats that can be edited with common editing tools such as Adobe Photoshop."

The first image below is an example of an equirectangular JPEG image. As you look toward the edges of the image, notice that the details get distorted. When the image is wrapped around a sphere, which is what happens after the image is imported into a development tool like CenarioVR, much of the distortion is eliminated. In the second image, you can see the picture after it is added to a scene in CenarioVR and an initial view has been set.

VR Cameras

What kind of camera do you need to create VR images and videos? Believe it or not, just about any standard 360 camera you can find at Best Buy or online at websites like amazon.com will work. The cameras are surprisingly inexpensive. For example, I recently purchased the Insta360 One X2 with a touchscreen, tripod, and loads of extras for less than $500. My first VR camera was the Insta360 Nano, and it cost less than $100. In the image below, the Insta360 One X2 is shown in the lower right-hand corner.

The GoProMax, pictured in the image above at the top right, is currently John's favorite because it's waterproof and he likes its software. However, John is quick to point out that "technology is moving very fast and my recommendation could change at any time."

John has written an informative article that compares images taken with different VR cameras. You can review the article by scanning the QR code below with your device.

Filming in 360

Filming with a 360 camera is similar to filming with your phone, dedicated camera, or video camera. However, there are things you need to take into account when creating 360 videos.

Unlike filming with regular cameras, everything in the viewfinder of a 360 camera—objects directly in front, behind, under, and above the camera—is being filmed.

When filming, find a hiding spot for yourself. Check out the image below. Can you find me?

In the image above, I'm hiding against the hay bales in the far stall. Kiki the cat appears to be walking toward the hay. In reality, she is curious about what I'm doing in my hiding place and is coming to investigate. I tried to distract Kiki, but failed. While I could have used Photoshop to remove Kiki from the image, I didn't have the heart.

While Kiki survived final edits, I noticed that part of my boot was visible in the original photo and I attempted to remove it. Sadly, my Photoshop skills are not the best. If it was possible for you to zoom closer to the image above, and I'm thankful that you cannot, you would see that I made a bit of a mess of the post between the two stalls.

There are two morals to my Kiki/Photoshop/hiding place story. First, scout out an appropriate hiding space in advance *and* give yourself enough time to get to your hiding place *before* the camera takes the picture. Alternatively, rather than dealing with a hiding place, you can intentionally include yourself in the shot by becoming one of the scene "actors," especially if you're taking a picture that includes a crowd.

The second moral of the story is that most 360 cameras come with a companion phone application that allows you to control the camera remotely. The camera used to take the image above didn't have this feature. On that first camera, pressing and holding the power button activated a five-second timer. I then had five seconds to run and hide. That's not an ideal situation, especially if the hiding space is narrow, you're wearing boots, you're slow, and there's a curious cat. The camera I use today includes the companion software and has cool features such as remote on/off, timer delay, and robust editing features.

The Roller-Coaster Effect vs. Teleporting

When you create a 360 video that allows the learner to glide through a scene or ride a roller-coaster, the effect seems cool at first—and it is. However, because of the possible and quite sudden shifts and jerking movements, the roller-coaster effect could make some of your learners nauseous.

Can you imagine the feedback you'll get after someone experiences the roller coaster effect in your VR training?

You: "How was the training, Bart?"

Bart: "It made me sick!"

Nice!

Instead of employing the roller-coaster effect, consider elegantly transporting your learner from scene to scene by adding clickable hotspots within a scene. You'll learn how to add hotspots beginning on page 22. They can be added to any scene. When the learner clicks a hotspot, an action can jump the learner from one scene to another. The brain perceives the scene jump as motion. However, the inner ear does not perceive the scene change as motion hence there isn't a chance for an upset stomach.

Camera Positioning

Your camera's perspective is going to end up being the learner's perspective. You should position the camera approximately four to five feet from the main subject. This distance gives the subject priority without getting too close.

The camera should be at eye level or just slightly above. It should be comfortable for the VR learner to look straight ahead, or even just slightly up. You do not want the camera set too high or too low because that leads to a floating feeling (if too high) or a pet's eye view (if too low) when you're trying to achieve total immersion for the learner.

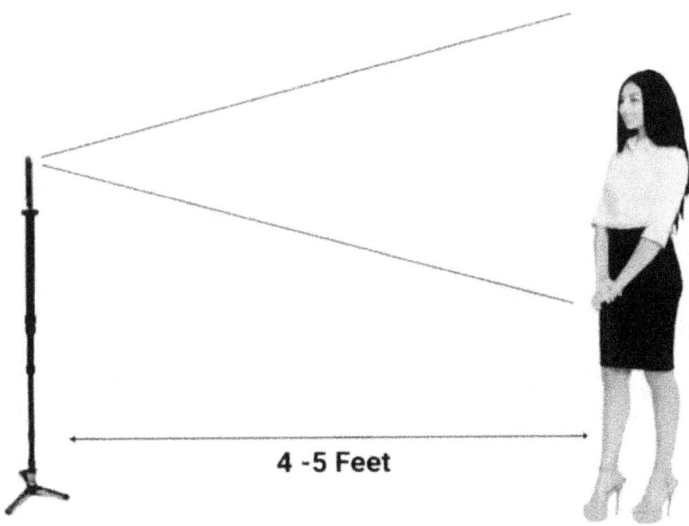

Stitching

VR 360 cameras have two lenses that each take up to a 210-degree semicircle image or video similar to what is shown below.

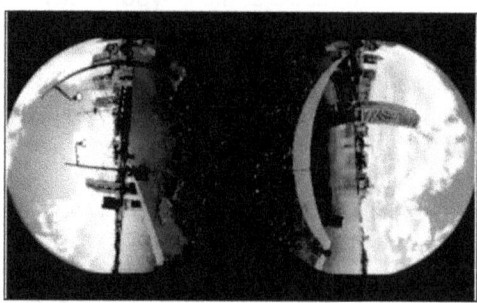

The VR cameras come with software that automatically puts the two pieces together based on complex matching algorithms. This process is known as **stitching**.

The quality of the stitching varies dependent upon the camera and the software.

From a practical standpoint, you don't want the learner to focus on the stitched areas—that's typically the 90 and 270 degree point from the front of the camera as shown at the right—because these areas are not as sharp as the rest of the image or video.

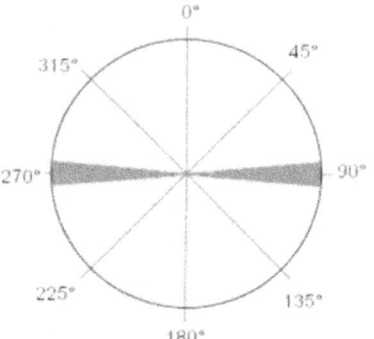

In the first image below, the stitching area is highlighted. The stitched portion of the image is not as sharp as the rest of the image. Is it terrible? No. But the difference is noticeable to the learner. The second image below was taken with a smartphone. The phone required several pictures to create the 360 image instead of the two needed by dedicated VR cameras. The extra pictures required extra stitches. And thanks to some poor stitching, the post appears split into two. Fixing the problem will require significant work in an editor like Photoshop.

Now that you've learned a little bit about 360-degree image essentials and what it will take to create your own assets, it's time to roll up the sleeves and dive into CenarioVR with hands-on lessons that begin on page 8.

"Skills and Drills" Learning

Module 1: Scenarios and Scenes

In This Module You Will Learn About:

- The CenarioVR Interface, page 8
- New Projects, page 13

And You Will Learn To:

- Import a Project into CenarioVR, page 8
- Explore the CenarioVR Interface, page 10
- Create a New Scenario and Add Scenes, page 13
- Manage Scenarios and Scenes, page 16

The CenarioVR Interface

CenarioVR projects begin with scenarios, a collection of scenes that can contain objects such as text, images, hotspots, and more. You can create an unlimited number of scenarios, each containing an unlimited numbers of scenes.

During the activities that follow, you'll access CenarioVR, create a new scenario, add scenes, images, and hotspots.

Guided Activity 1: Import a Project into CenarioVR

1. Access CenarioVR.

   ☐ using a web browser, go to **www.cenariovr.com**

   ☐ click **Login**

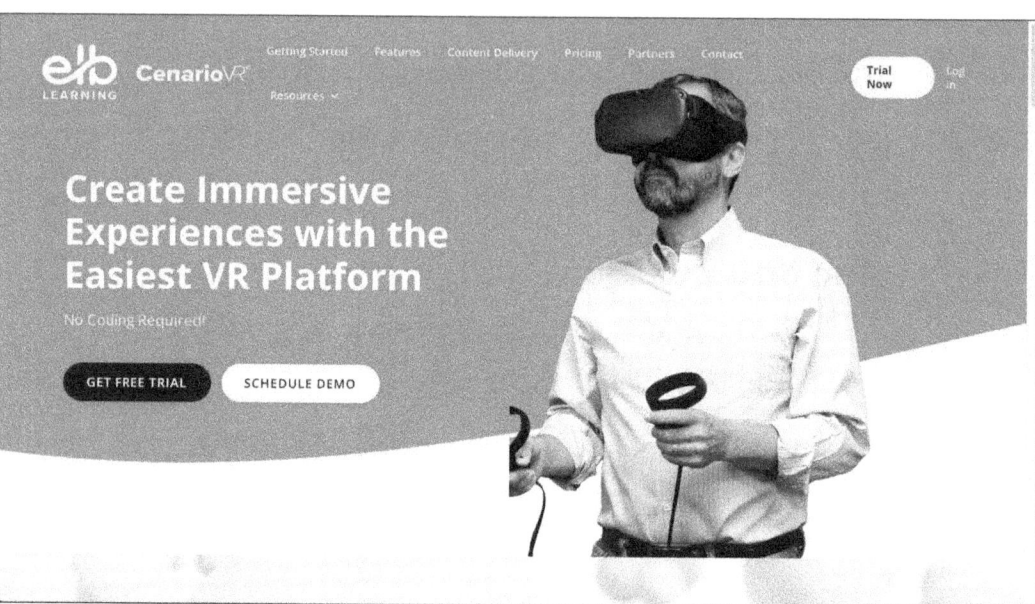

While you can use CenarioVR on desktop computers, laptops, tablets, or smartphones, I found the development experience best on a desktop or laptop. The screenshots shown in this book were taken on my MacBook Pro. Because the CenarioVR interface is responsive, your screen may look different from what is shown in this book.

☐ login to CenarioVR using your email address and password (note that if you do not have a CenarioVR account, a free trial is available)

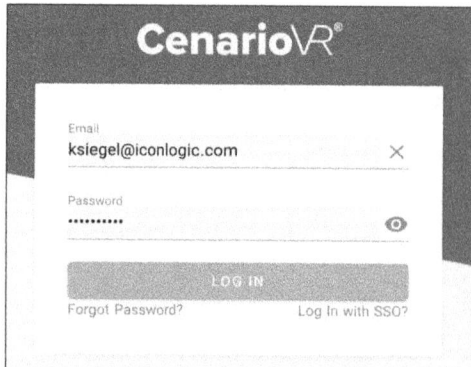

Module 1: Scenarios and Scenes > The CenarioVR Interface > Import a Project into CenarioVR

2. Import a completed project CenarioVR.
   - ☐ from the upper-right of the screen, use your mouse and hover above the **plus sign**
   - ☐ click **Import Scenario**

   - ☐ click the **Upload** icon and, from the **CVRData** folder, open the **scenarios** folder
   - ☐ open **ChesapeakeStablesTour.zip**

The project is imported and appears in the **My Scenarios area**. Because CenarioVR is a cloud-based application, your project is saved automatically to the CenarioVR server as you work. You'll learn how to export CenarioVR projects to your computer later—a great way to ensure you always have a backup of your project and its assets saved locally.

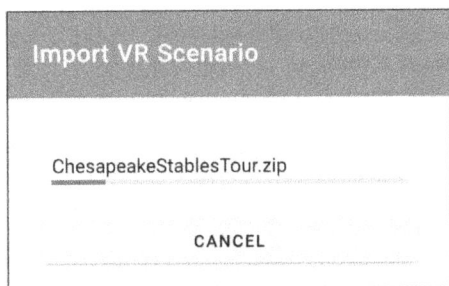

   - ☐ if necessary, click **My Scenarios** to see a thumbnail of the uploaded project.

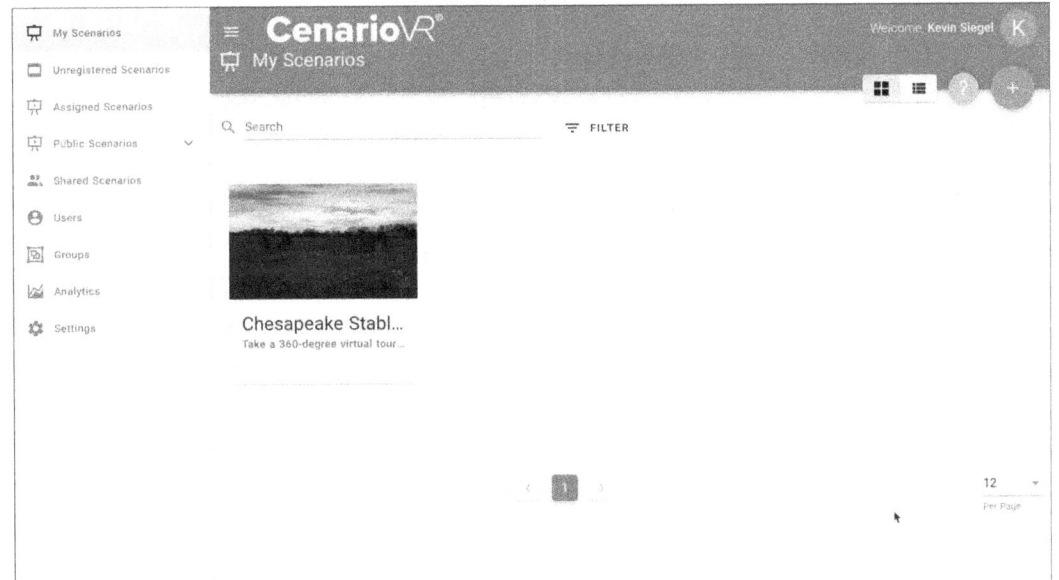

Guided Activity 2: Explore the CenarioVR Interface

1. Open a Scenario.

   ☐ from the **My Scenarios** area, double-click the **Chesapeake Stables** scenario that you just uploaded

At the left is the scene list. Each scene is represented by a thumbnail image. Each scene contains multiple objects listed beneath the thumbnail image. The first scene, named **Barn Entrance**, is open. In the middle of the screen you can see the editor, also known as the canvas, where you'll do most of your CenarioVR development work.

2. Switch between scenes.

   ☐ from the list of scenes, click the second thumbnail image

You can only work in one scene at a time. As the Aisle A scene opens, the Barn Entrance scene closes automatically. The editor window changes to display the second scene and the list of Aisle A scene assets appears beneath the scene's thumbnail image.

3. Explore a scene.

   ☐ from the **scene list**, select the **Barn Entrance** scene

   The scene contains a 360-degree image, the barn's logo, text, a start button, and two hotspots allowing for entry into the barn.

   ☐ drag the editor window right

   The editor window contains a 360-degree image so you can drag up, down, left, right... all directions. As you drag right, you'll come across two hotspots positioned over the two barn doors. You'll learn how to add these kinds of assets soon.

4. Preview the project.

   ☐ at the upper right of the window, click the **Preview Mode** icon (the eyeball)

   While in Preview mode, the CenarioVR development tools disappear. You're seeing the scene as it would appear to your end-users. You can hear the scene's voiceover audio and the hotspots are now clickable.

5. Return to Edit mode.

   ☐ at the upper right of the window, click the **Pencil** icon to exit Preview mode

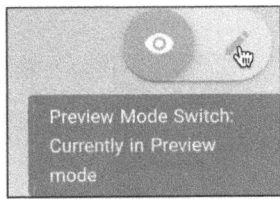

   The development tools reappear.

CenarioVR: The Essentials (Second Edition)

NOTES

Preview Confidence Check

As you move through the lessons in this book, you'll learn how to create the Chesapeake Stables project from scratch.

1. Return to Preview mode.
2. Click the **Start** button and notice that you are automatically panned right so you can see the two hotspots.
3. Click either hotspot to enter the barn.
4. Spend a few moments exploring the finished project.

   In particular, notice the interactive elements in the Aisle A Tack Room (including a quiz), the link to a YouTube video in Aisle A, and the drag and drop interaction in the Arena.

5. Close the preview.
6. Close the scenario by clicking the CenarioVR logo.

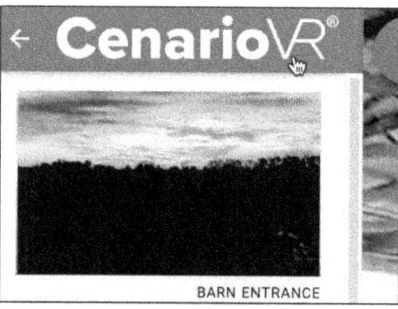

7. At the top right of the window, click the **two view icons** to switch between **List View** and **Grid View**.

   The view you choose is a personal preference and does not affect the functionality of CenarioVR.

Module 1: Scenarios and Scenes > New Projects > Create a New Scenario and Add Scenes

New Projects

Creating new projects—scenarios—in CenarioVR is as simple as clicking the plus sign in the upper right of the editor. Of course, prior to creating a new project, you'll need your 360 images and/or videos, scene images, and audio files. You don't have to worry about any of those assets as you use this book. I have provided everything you need amongst the data files that you downloaded in the **About This Book** section (see page viii). CenarioVR also comes with a helpful library of images, icons, and other assets you can use in your projects.

Guided Activity 3: Create a New Scenario and Add Scenes

1. Create a new scenario.

    ☐ from the upper-right of the CenarioVR window, click the **plus sign**

    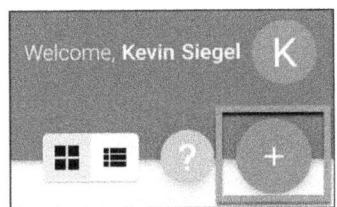

    The Create New VR Scenario screen opens.

    ☐ from the **Drop file here or click to upload** area, click the **upload** icon
    ☐ from the **CVRData** folder, open **images and videos**
    ☐ open **Retail1.jpg**
    ☐ in the **Description** area, type **Learning to add scenes, images, and hotspots.**

    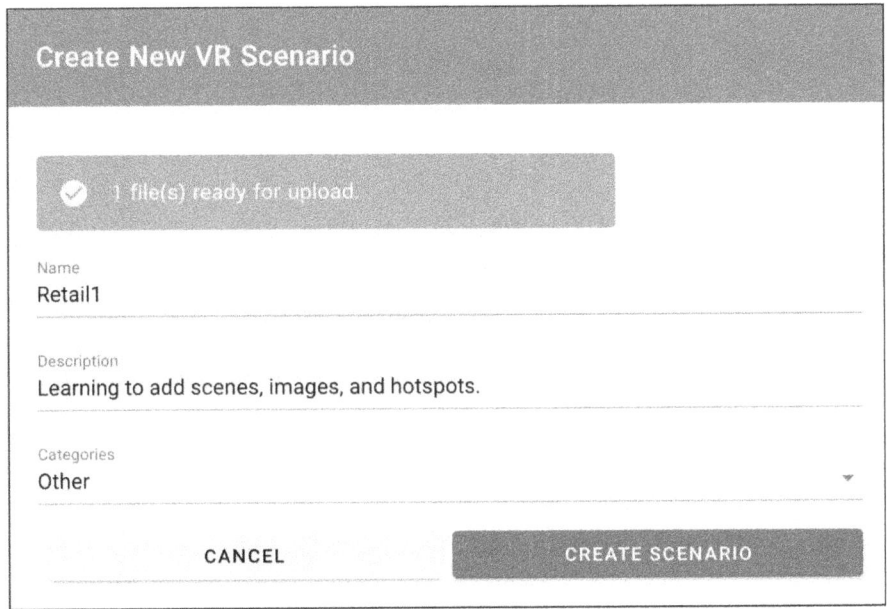

    ☐ click the **Create Scenario** button

    And just like that, you've created your first virtual reality project. On the **scenes** list, notice there's a single scene (named RETAIL1 after the image you uploaded).

NOTES

2. Add a new scene to the scenario.

   ☐ from beneath the **RETAIL1** scene, click **Add Scene** icon

The Scene window opens.

☐ from the **Drop file here or click to upload** area, click the **upload** icon

☐ from the **CVRData** folder, open **images and videos**

☐ open **Retail2.jpg**

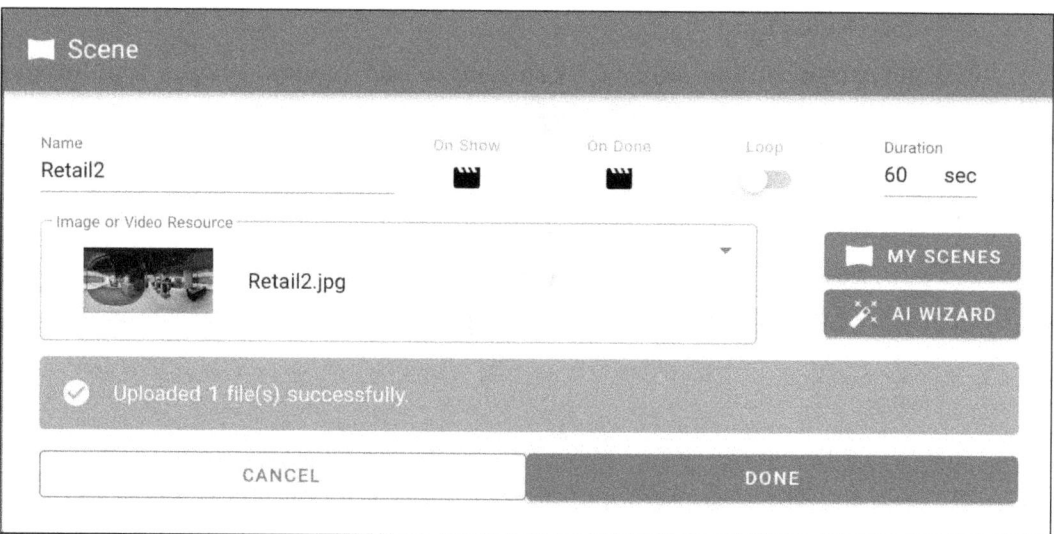

☐ click the **Done** button

Your scenario now contains two scenes: RETAIL1 and RETAIL2.

Module 1: Scenarios and Scenes > New Projects > Create a New Scenario and Add Scenes

3. Use the AI Wizard to create a scene.
   - ☐ from beneath the **RETAIL2** scene, click **Add Scene** icon
   - ☐ from the right side of the Scene dialog box, click the **AI Wizard** button
   - ☐ in the **Scene Description** field, type **Four mice sitting around a table playing poker.**
   - ☐ from the **Select Category** drop-down menu, choose any category that you like (note that I left my category set to the default, **Realism**)

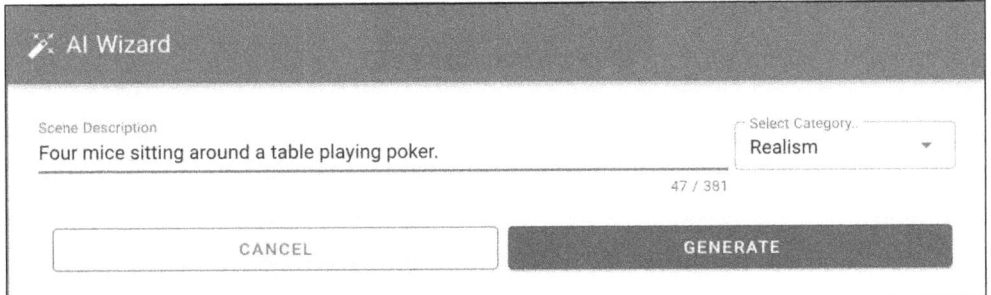

   - ☐ click the **Generate** button

   In a matter of seconds, the AI Wizard creates a stunning, 360-degree scene.

   - ☐ click the **Use** button
   - ☐ click the **Done** button to add the new scene to your scenario

4. Preview the scene. When finished, return to Edit mode.

5. Click the CenarioVR logo to close the scenario and return to the My Scenarios screen.

Guided Activity 4: Manage Scenarios and Scenes

1. Edit a Scenario's name and description.

   ☐ from the **My Scenarios** screen, point to the **Retail1 thumbnail** and click the **menu** (the three dots) in the upper right corner of the thumbnail

   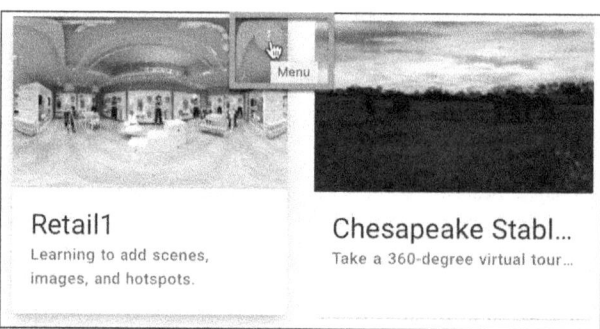

   ☐ click **Scenario Settings**

   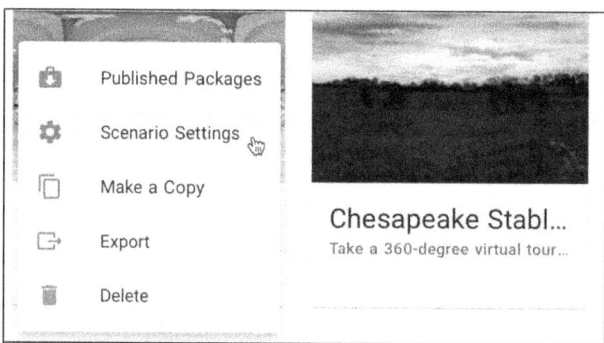

   ☐ change the name of the scenario to **Mall of the Universe**

   ☐ change the Description to **2,000 stores and one million square feet of awesomeness!**

   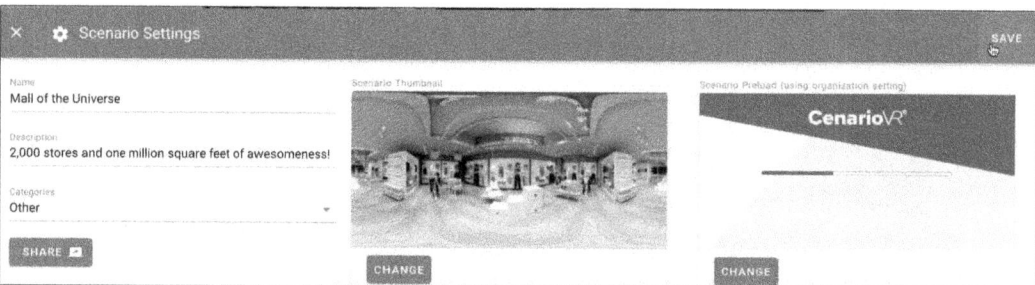

   ☐ from the **upper right** of the Scenario Settings, click **Save**

Module 1: Scenarios and Scenes > New Projects > Manage Scenarios and Scenes

2. Edit Scene names.
   - ☐ on the **My Scenarios** screen, double-click **Mall of the Universe** to open the scenario
   - ☐ from the **Scenes** list, click the first scene (RETAIL1)
   - ☐ from the top of the thumbnail image, click the **Pencil** icon

   The Scene Properties open.

   - ☐ change the **Name** to **Clothes! Clothes! Clothes!**

   - ☐ click the **Done** button

   - ☐ from the **Scenes** list, click the second scene (RETAIL2)
   - ☐ from the top of the thumbnail image, click the **Pencil** icon

   The Scene Properties reopen.

   - ☐ change the **Name** to **YoungN Hip**
   - ☐ click the **Done** button

3. Delete a Scenario.

    ☐ click the **CenarioVR logo** to return to the **My Scenarios** screen
    ☐ click the menu for the Mall of the Universe scenario

    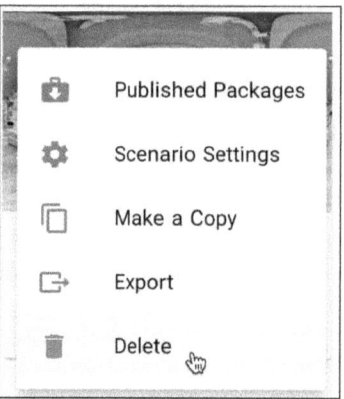

    ☐ click **Delete**

    Because you cannot recover a deleted scenario, you are required to confirm the deletion.

    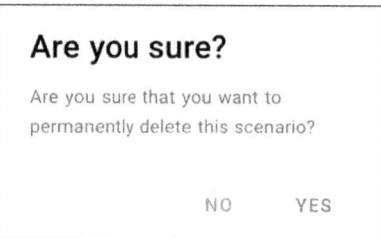

    ☐ click **Yes**

    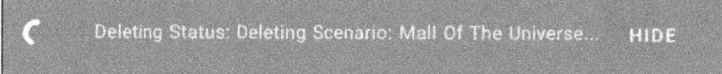

Module 1: Scenarios and Scenes > New Projects > Manage Scenarios and Scenes

New Scenarios and Scenes Confidence Check

1. Create a New scenario named **My Horse Stables** with the following Description: **Take a 360-degree virtual tour of our facility.**

   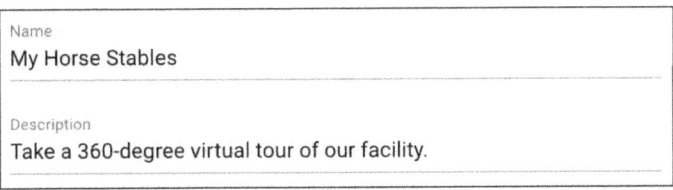

2. From **CVRData > images and videos,** upload **BarnEntrance.jpg** and finish creating the scenario per the image shown below.

   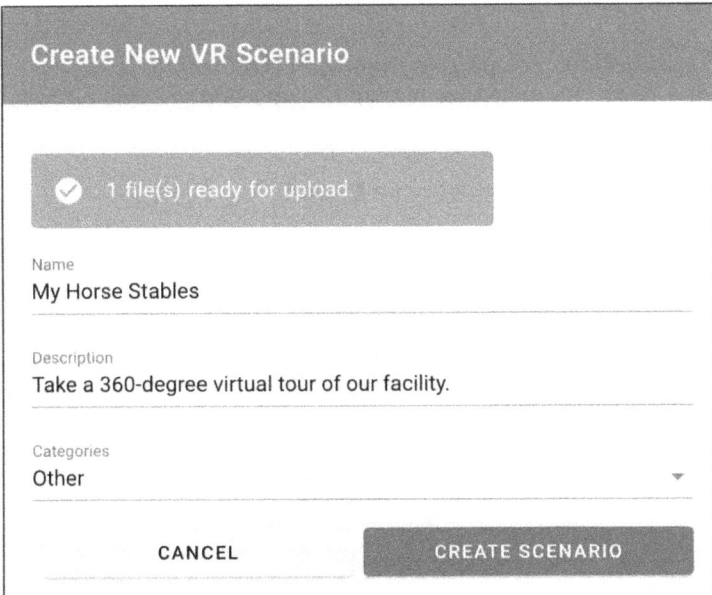

3. Make a slight edit to the scene's name by adding a space between the words **Barn** and **Entrance**.

   Note: You are limited to the number of scenes you can add to CenarioVR if you're using the trial. If you are unable to add scenes as instructed below, add as many as you can.

4. Add a new scene named **Aisle A** that uses the **AisleA.jpg**.
5. Add a new scene named **Tack Room** that uses the **TackRoom.jpg**.
6. Add a new scene named **Visitor Room** that uses the **VisitorRoom.jpg**.

NOTES

7. Add a new scene named **Indoor Arena** that uses the **Arena.jpg**.
8. Add a new scene named **Aisle B** that uses the **AisleB.jpg**.
9. Add a new scene named **Parking Lot** that also uses the **BarnEntrance.jpg**.

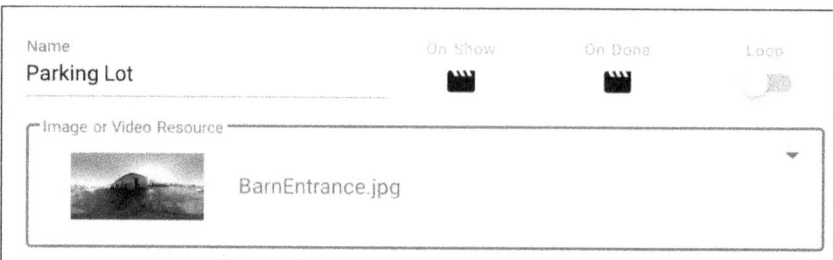

10. Return to the **My Scenarios** screen.

    Note: You cannot export scenarios nor publish them with the CenarioVR trial. If you are using the trial, review the next step but it's unlikely that you will be able to complete it.

11. Click the menu for **My Horse Stables** and choose **Export**.

    The exported project and its assets are zipped and saved to your computer (typically to the **Downloads** folder). This zipped project can be re-imported into CenarioVR or used as a local backup.

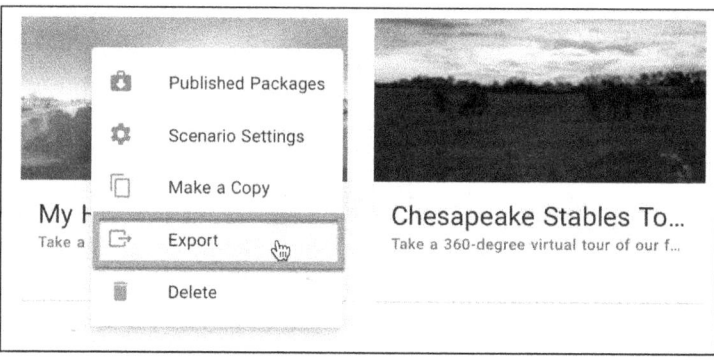

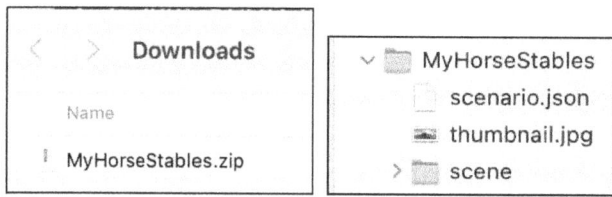

"Skills and Drills" Learning

Module 2: Hotspots, Info Cards, and Images

In This Module You Will Learn About:

- Hotspots, page 22
- Info Cards, page 27
- Images, page 29
- Initial Views, page 30
- Image and Transparent Hotspots, page 31

And You Will Learn To:

- Import a Project, page 22
- Add a Hotspot, page 23
- Add a Hotspot Action, page 25
- Add an Info Card, page 27
- Add an Image, page 29
- Set the Initial View, page 30
- Add an Image Hotspot, page 31
- Edit a Hotspot Action, page 33
- Add a Transparent Hotspot, page 34

Hotspots

Hotspots allow your learner to interact with and move through your virtual reality project. During the next few activities, you'll import a project, learn how to add hotspots to icons, transparent hotpots, and set hotspot actions.

Guided Activity 5: Import a Project

1. Ensure that you are logged into CenarioVR and on the **My Scenarios** screen.

2. Import a project.

   ☐ from the upper-right of the screen, use your mouse and hover above the **plus sign**

   ☐ click **Import Scenario**

   ☐ click the **Upload** icon and, from the **CVRData** folder, open the **scenarios** folder

   ☐ open **HotspotMe.zip**

   The project is imported and appears in the My Scenarios area.

Guided Activity 6: Add a Hotspot

1. Open the HotspotMe scenario.

    ☐ double-click the words **HotspotMe**

2. Add a hotspot onto a scene.

    ☐ click the the **Barn Entrance** scene

    ☐ if necessary, drag the editor window so that you can see the main barn door entrance

    ☐ click the **Add Object** icon

    ☐ click **Add Hotspot**

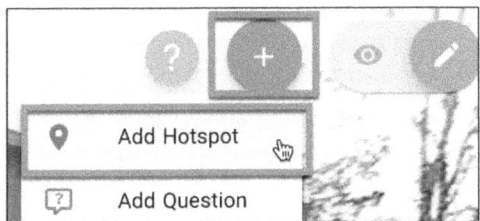

The Hotspot options open.

    ☐ click the **Media Library** button
    ☐ select **ICONS**
    ☐ expand the **Image** group

    ☐ double-click the **adjust** icon to add it as the hotspot

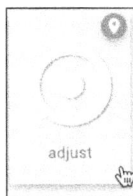

- [ ] back in the **Hotspot** window, change the name of the hotspot to **Barn door hotspot**

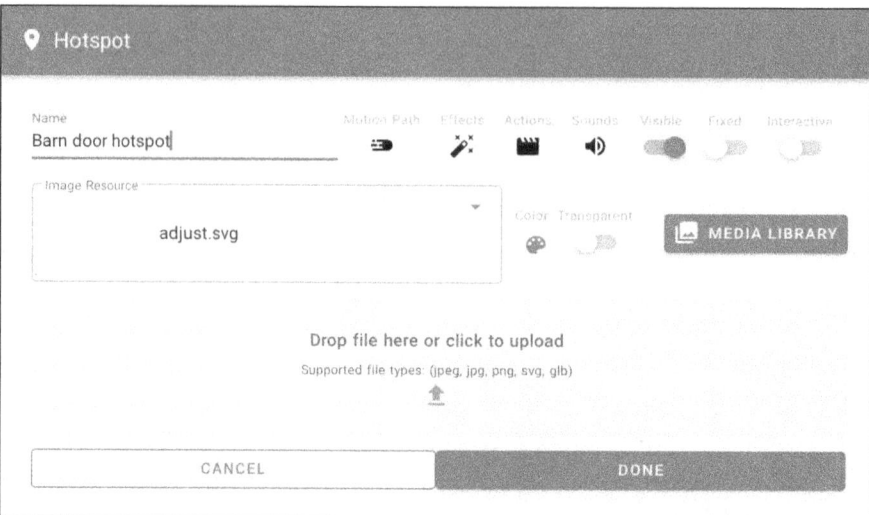

- [ ] click the **Done** button
- [ ] position the hotspot over the barn door entrance as shown in the image below

3. Test the hotspot.

    - [ ] switch to **Preview** mode

    - [ ] click the hotspot

    Because you have not yet defined a hotspot action, nothing happens when you click the hotspot.

    - [ ] return to **Edit** mode

Guided Activity 7: Add a Hotspot Action

1. Ensure that you're still working in the **Barn Entrance** scene of the **HotspotMe** scenario and in **Edit** mode.

2. Add an action to a hotspot.

   ☐ on the Canvas, **double-click** the **Barn door hotspot**

   The Hotspot properties reopen.

   ☐ click **Actions**

   The Hotspot actions open.

   ☐ from the **Action** area, click **Choose An Action**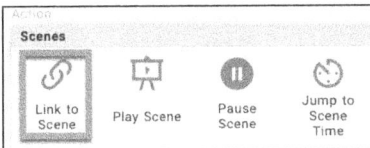

   ☐ from the **Scenes** area, click **Link to Scene**

   ☐ from the Scenes drop-down menu, choose **Aisle A**

   ☐ click **Back To Properties**

   Notice that the **Actions** icon is labeled with a **1**, indicating that you've added an action to the object. As you will learn later, you can add multiple—even conditional—actions to any object.

   ☐ click the **Done** button

3. Test the hotspot.

   ☐ switch to **Preview** mode

   ☐ click the hotspot

Clicking the hotspot should take you to the Aisle A scene.

☐ return to **Edit** mode

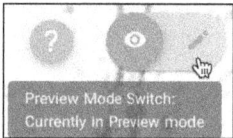

Notice that you're now on the Aisle A scene.

4. Return to the Barn Entrance scene.

Info Cards

Info Cards are similar to text boxes in Microsoft PowerPoint or text captions and callouts in eLearning tools like Adobe Captivate or Articulate Storyline. Once added to a scene, you can format the card's font, size, text color, and color opacity.

Guided Activity 8: Add an Info Card

1. Ensure that you're still in the **HotspotMe** scenario.

2. Add an Info Card.

    ☐ on the **Barn Entrance** scene, click the **Add Object** icon

    ☐ click **Add Info Card**

    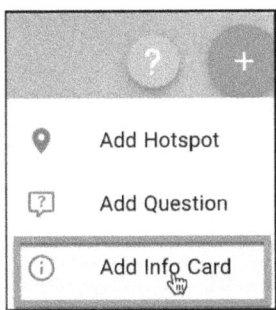

    The Info Card options open.

    ☐ name the Info Card **Welcome Text**

    ☐ type the following into the Info Card Text area: **Welcome to Chesapeake Stables. The barn entrance is to your right.**

    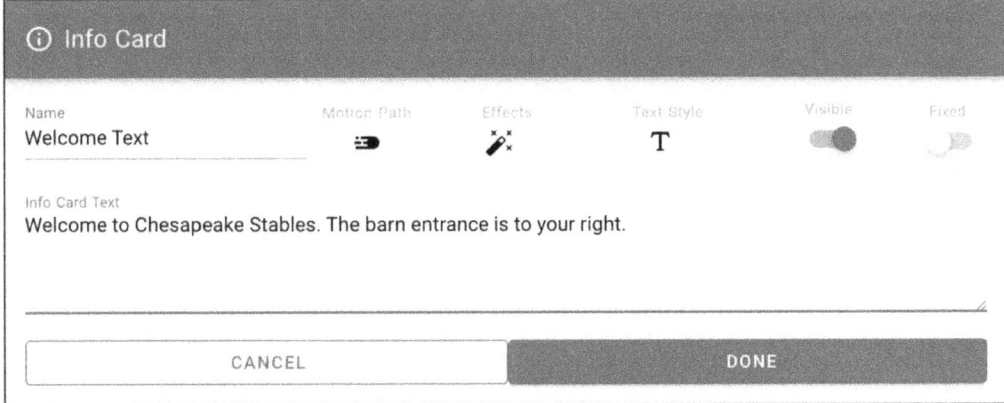

    ☐ click the **Done** button

    The Info Card appears onscreen covering the hotspot and part of the door.

3. Change the text style used in the Info Card.

    ☐ double-click the **Info Card**

    The Info Card options reopen.

NOTES

☐ click **Text Style**

The Info Card text styles screen opens.

☐ from the **Font** menu, select any font you like

☐ from the **Card Color** area, select any color you like

☐ click **Back to Properties**

☐ click the **Done** button

Note: Text formatting can also be made using the toolbar that appears at the top of the window when you select the Info Card.

4. Drag the Info Card left and position it similar to what is shown in the image below.

Module 2: Hotspots, Info Cards, and Images > Images > Add an Image

Images

In addition to accepting 360 images and videos, there is a media library that contains icons and 3D models that you can use in any scene. And CenarioVR allows you to import jpg, png, and svg images from your computer. During the activities that follow, you'll upload an image for use on the Barn Entrance scene. Later, you'll add a 3D image of a horse to the Indoor Arena scene.

Guided Activity 9: Add an Image

1. Ensure that you're still working in the **Barn Entrance** scene of the **HotspotMe** scenario.

2. Import an image.

   ☐ click the **Add Object** icon

   ☐ click **Add Image**

   The Image options open.

   ☐ click the **Upload** icon

   ☐ from **CVRData** > **images and videos**, open **ChesapeakeStablesLogo.png**

   ☐ edit the Name slightly to **Chesapeake Stables Logo** (add spaces between the words)

   ☐ click the **Done** button

3. Position and resize the image similar to what is shown in the screenshot below.

Initial Views

When a learner first enters a scene, they're seeing a default initial view. You can easily control what the learner sees by editing the initial view. And as you'll learn during a confidence check later, initial views can also be controlled by hotspot actions.

Guided Activity 10: Set the Initial View

1. Click the CenarioVR logo to return to the My Scenario's screen.

2. Open **HotspotMe** scenario.

   Notice that when you open the scene, your initial view is the entrance to the barn instead of the welcome text and the logo. You can control what the learner sees when a scene is first opened by setting the initial view.

3. Set the Initial View.

   ☐ on the **Scenes** list, hover above the thumbnail image for the **Barn Entrance**

   ☐ click the **Set Initial View** icon

   ☐ drag the Canvas **left** until the view looks similar to what is shown below

   ☐ click the **Done** button

4. Click the CenarioVR logo to return to the My Scenario's screen.

5. Reopen **HotspotMe** scenario.

   The initial view is now set to display the welcome text Info Card and the Chesapeake Stables logo.

Module 2: Hotspots, Info Cards, and Images > Image and Transparent Hotspots > Add an Image Hotspot

Image and Transparent Hotspots

You have previously learned how to use icons as hotspots. However, you can upload and use any image as a hotspot. In addition, you can make a hotspot transparent and transform any portion of the Canvas into an interactive area.

Guided Activity 11: Add an Image Hotspot

1. Ensure that you're still working in the **Barn Entrance** scene of the **HotspotMe** scenario.

2. Use an image as a hotspot.

    ☐ click the **Add Object** icon

    ☐ click **Add Hotspot**

    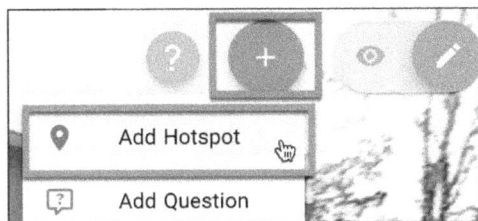

    The Hotspot options open.

    ☐ click the **Upload** icon and, from **CVRData > images and videos**, open **StartButton.png**

    ☐ name the Hotspot **Start Button** (add the space between the words)

    ☐ click **Actions** and then click **Choose An Action**

    ☐ click **Link to Scene**

    ☐ from the **Scenes** drop-down menu, choose **Aisle A**

    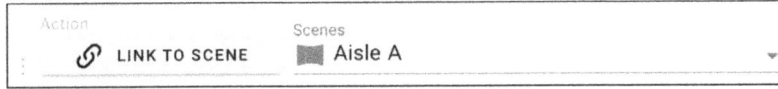

    ☐ click **Back to Properties**

    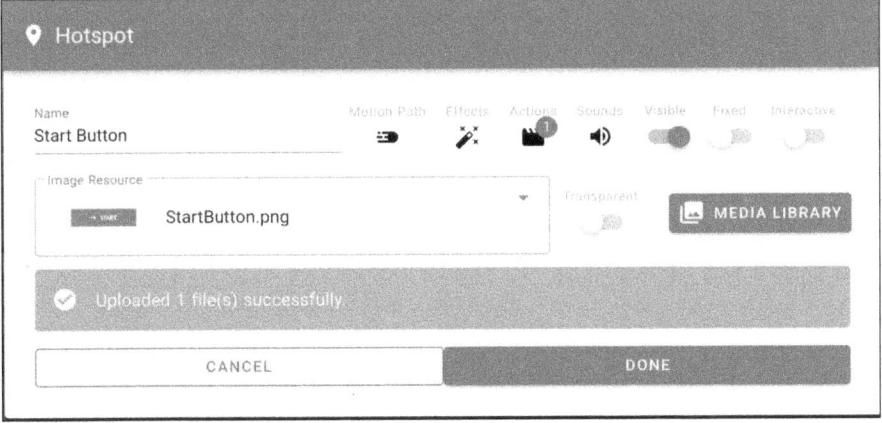

    ☐ click the **Done** button

3. Position the Start button similar to what is shown in the image below.

4. Test the hotspot.

☐ switch to **Preview** mode

☐ click the **Start** button

You are taken to the Aisle A scene as expected. However, it would be slicker if clicking the Start button panned to the hotspot in front of the barn door. You'll use the Pan action to take care of that next.

☐ return to **Edit** mode

Module 2: Hotspots, Info Cards, and Images > Image and Transparent Hotspots > Edit a Hotspot Action

Guided Activity 12: Edit a Hotspot Action

1. Ensure that you're still working in the **HotspotMe** scenario.

2. Edit a hotspot action so that it uses the Pan feature.

   ☐ if necessary, switch to the **Barn Entrance** scene
   ☐ on the Canvas, double-click the **Start** button
   ☐ click **Actions**
   ☐ click **Link To Scene**
   ☐ from the **Object Actions** area, select **Pan To**
   ☐ from the **Objects** drop-down menu, choose **Barn door hotspot**

   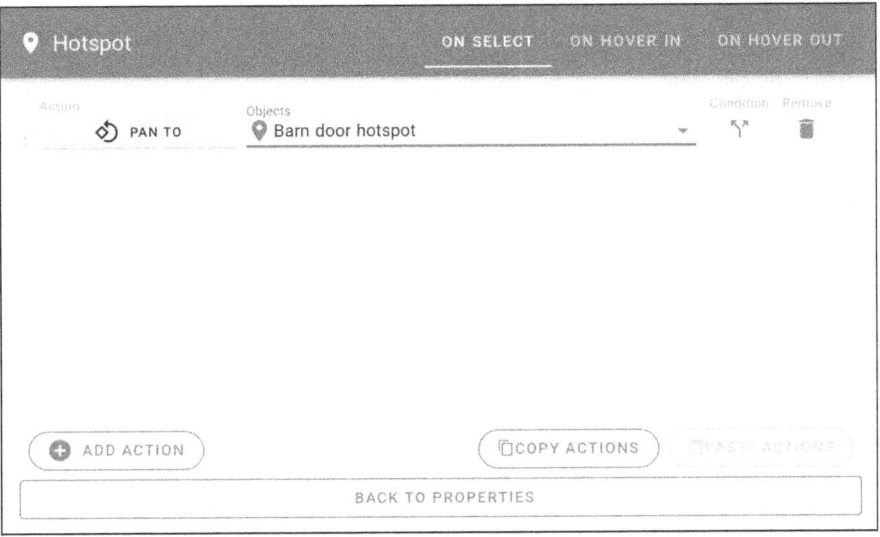

   ☐ click **Back to Properties**
   ☐ click the **Done** button

3. Test the hotspot.

   ☐ switch to **Preview** mode
   ☐ click the **Start** button

   This time, you are panned elegantly to the Barn Entrance hotspot.

   ☐ return to **Edit** mode

   Note: I think panning is a cool effect and because most of my learners will be accessing my courses over the web, I plan to use the feature a lot. However, according to the ELB Learning, "panning can be disorienting to learners using a headset. Small amounts of panning are fine, but anything that takes headset learners more than 50 or 60 degrees around a scene should be avoided."

Guided Activity 13: Add a Transparent Hotspot

1. Open the **Aisle A** scene of the **HotspotMe** scenario.

2. Insert a transparent hotspot that opens a web link.

    ☐ click the **Add Object** icon

    ☐ click **Add Hotspot**

    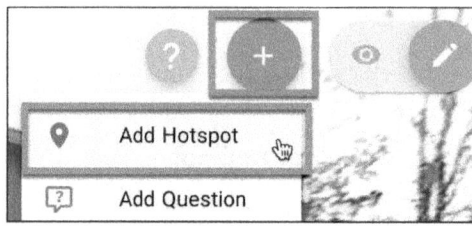

    The Hotspot options open.

    ☐ click **Transparent**

    ☐ click **Actions** and then click **Choose An Action**

    ☐ from the **Web** area, click **Web Link**

    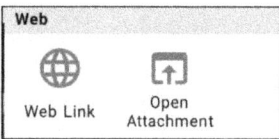

    ☐ review and acknowledge the web link limitations by clicking the **OK** button

    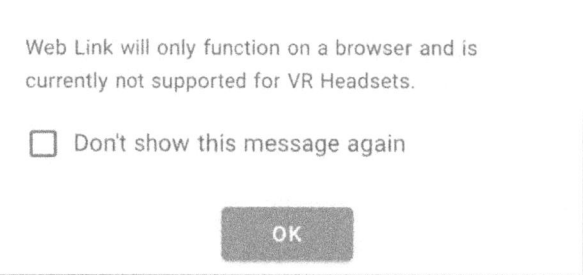

    ☐ type the following into the URL area:
    https://www.youtube.com/watch?v=dsDvDoikYCk

    ☐ click **Back to Properties**

    ☐ click **Done**

Hotspots Confidence Check

1. Move and resize the transparent hotspot over the hay, similar to what is shown in the image below.

2. Preview the scene and test the web link.
3. Return to Edit mode and select the Barn Entrance scene.
4. Add a hotspot using the **adjust.svg** icon over the smaller door in front of the barn entrance that links to the **Aisle B** scene.

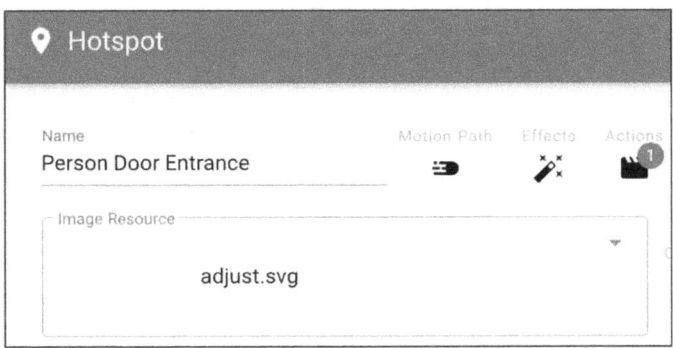

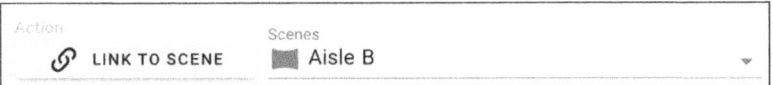

5. Open the **Aisle A** scene.
6. Add a hotspot using the **adjust.svg** icon at the end of the aisle that links to the **Indoor Arena** scene.

   Note: The default color of the indoor arena hotspot is white. A darker color would make the hotspot easier to see. You can change the color of a hotspot icon via the Color option available in the Hotspot properties screen.

   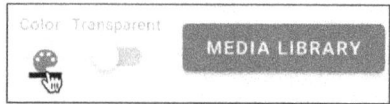

7. Open the Indoor Arena scene.
8. Add a hotspot that goes back to the Aisle A scene.

9. Preview the Indoor Arena scene.

   When you click the hotspot to go back to Aisle A, the orientation is set as if you've entered the aisle from the main barn door, which is incorrect. It should appear as if you entered the aisle from the other direction.

10. Edit the hotspot's action and click the **Scene Direction** icon.

11. Drag the scene until the orientation is similar to the image below.

12. Preview the Indoor Arena scene again.

    This time, when you click the hotspot to go back Aisle A, the orientation is set as if you've left the arena and are heading down the aisle, back toward the entrance. *How cool is that?*

13. Still working in the Indoor Arena scene, add the horse **3D Model** object from the Media Library.

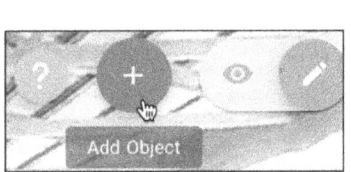 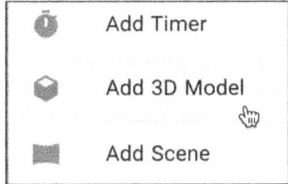

14. Resize and position the horse similar to the image below.

15. Spend a few minutes adding hotspots that will allow your learners to move from aisle to aisle and room to room.

    Note: This is an opportunity for you to play with hotspots and increase your confidence. Because you will soon be importing a project with all of the scene to scene hotspots added, there is no need to build out all of the hotspots.

16. Change the colors of the hotspots as appropriate.
17. Change the Scene Direction for the hotspots as appropriate.
18. Preview the project and test your hotspots.
19. When ready to move on, click the CenarioVR logo to return to the My Scenario's screen.

"Skills and Drills" Learning

Module 3: Audio, Groups, and Conditional Actions

In This Module You Will Learn About:

- Audio, page 40
- Grouping, page 50
- Conditional Actions, page 55

And You Will Learn To:

- Add Audio to a Scene, page 40
- Attach Audio to an Object, page 43
- Control Object Visibility, page 46
- Add an Info Card and Image Hotspots, page 50
- Group Objects, page 53
- Create IF/AND Conditions, page 55
- Create IF/OR Conditions, page 58

Audio

In my experience, adding audio to a project, especially voiceover audio, enhances the learner experience. While you cannot record audio with CenarioVR, you can import existing MP3 files onto a scene and control such things as when it plays, its volume, and what event—if any—occurs when the audio completes.

> **Note:** MP3 (MPEG Audio Layer 3) files are compressed digital audio files. MP3 files are often a fraction of the size of an uncompressed WAVE or AIFF file, but have about the same audio quality as uncompressed formats.

Guided Activity 14: Add Audio to a Scene

1. Ensure that you are logged into CenarioVR and on the **My Scenarios** screen.

2. Import the **AudioGroupConditionMe.zip** project from **CVRData > scenarios**. (If you need help, refer to the "Import a Project into CenarioVR" activity that begins on page 8.)

3. Open the **AudioGroupConditionMe** scenario.

4. Add voiceover audio to a scene.

   ☐ with the **Barn Entrance** scene open, click the **Add Object** icon

   ☐ click **Add Audio**

   The Audio dialog box opens.

   ☐ click the **Upload** icon

   ☐ from **CVRData > audio**, open **welcome.mp3**

   ☐ name the file **Welcome Audio**

   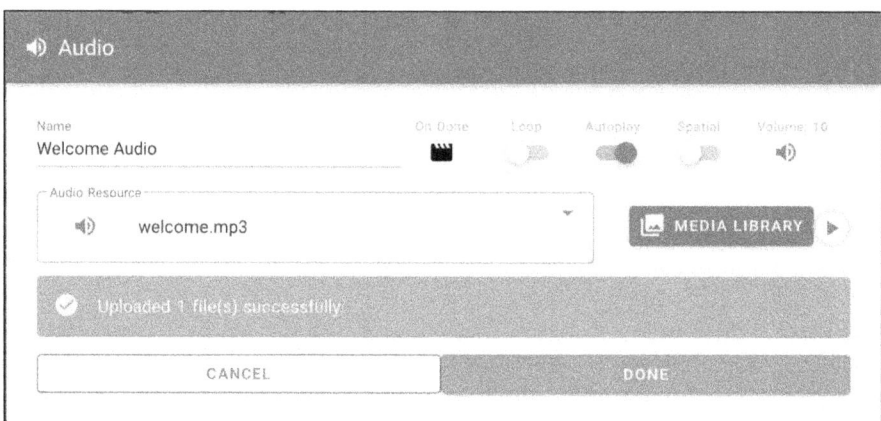

   ☐ click the **Done** button

5. Preview the audio.

   ☐ switch to **Preview** mode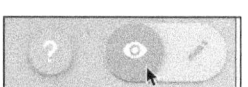

   The welcome audio plays as expected. In the next step, you'll add an action that immediately stops the audio if the Start button is clicked.

6. Return to **Edit** mode.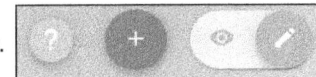

7. Add an action to a button that disables the audio.

   ☐ on the Canvas, double-click the **Start** button

   The Hotspot dialog box opens.

   ☐ click **Actions**

   ☐ from the **bottom left** of the Hotspot screen, click **Add Action**

   ☐ click **Choose An Action**

   ☐ from the **Audio, Video and Timers** area, click **Stop**

   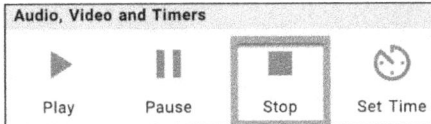

   ☐ from the **Objects** drop-down menu, choose **Welcome Audio**

   ☐ click **Back to Properties**
   ☐ click **Done**

Audio Confidence Check

1. Preview the scene and, before the voiceover audio finishes, click the Start button.

   The audio stops the instant you click the Start button.

2. Return to Edit mode.

3. Open the **Aisle A** scene.

4. Add the **aisleAAudio** audio file onto the scene and name the file **Aisle A Audio**.

5. Preview the scene to hear the audio.

6. Return to Edit mode.

7. Open the **Parking Lot** scene.

8. Add the **thanks** audio file onto the scene, name the audio **Thanks audio**.

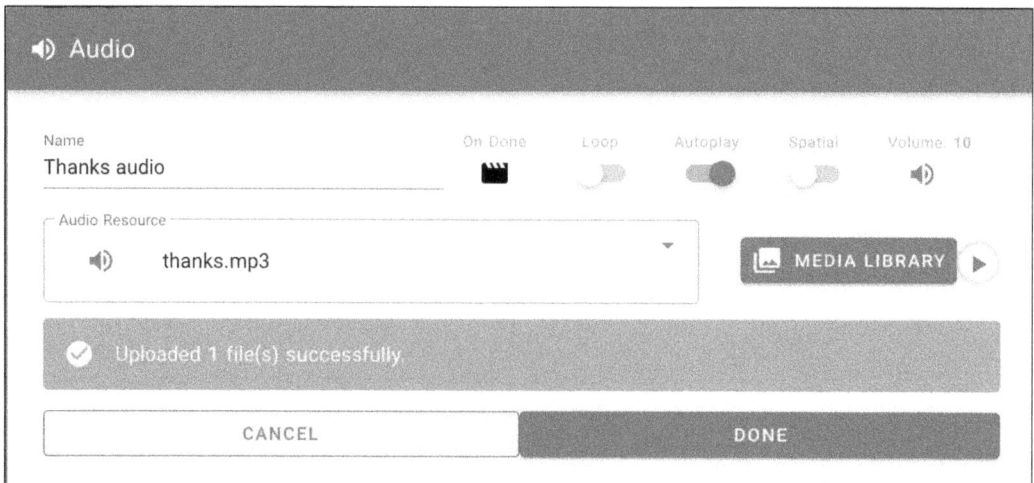

9. Click the **Play** icon to the right of Media Library to preview the audio.

10. Click the **Done** button.

Module 3: Audio, Groups, and Conditional Actions > Audio > Attach Audio to an Object

Guided Activity 15: Attach Audio to an Object

1. Ensure that the **AudioGroupConditionMe** scenario is open.

2. Open the **Aisle A** scene.

   Notice that here are audio and stop hotspot icons that will soon control the scene's voiceover audio. (You learned how to insert hotspots onto a scene beginning on page 23.)

3. Preview the scene and notice that the scene's audio plays automatically. You will disable the audio for a moment so that it can be controlled by the scene's audio hotspot.

4. Return to Edit mode.

5. Disable Audio Autoplay.

   ☐ from the list of Aisle A scene assets below the scene, select **AisleAAudio**

   ☐ click the **Edit** icon

   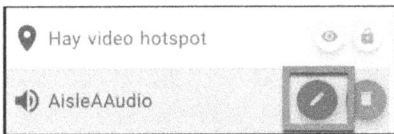

   The Audio dialog box opens.

   ☐ in the **Autoplay** area, click the slider to disable the option

   ☐ click the **Done** button

6. Preview the scene and notice that this time the audio does not automatically play.

7. Return to Edit mode.

8. Add a Play audio action to a hotspot.

   ☐ still working on the **Aisle A** scene, from the list of scene assets below the scene, select **Play Aisle A Audio**

   Note: The Play Aisle A Audio item is the hotspot on the scene near the cat.

☐ click the **Edit** icon

The Hotspot options open.

☐ click **Actions**

☐ ensure that the **On Select** tab is selected

☐ click **Add Action** and then click **Choose An Action**

☐ from the **Audio, Video and Timers** area, click **Play**

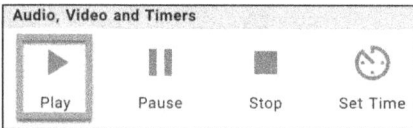

☐ from the **Objects** drop-down menu, choose **AisleAAudio**

☐ click **Back to Properties**

☐ click **Done**

9. Add a Stop Audio action to a hotspot.

☐ still working on the **Aisle A** scene, from the list of scene assets at the left, select **Stop Audio**

☐ click the **Edit** icon

The Hotspot options reopen.

☐ click **Actions**

☐ ensure that **On Select** is selected

☐ click **Add Action**

☐ click **Choose An Action**

☐ from the **Audio, Video and Timers** area, click **Stop**

☐ from the **Objects** drop-down menu, choose **AisleAAudio**

☐ click **Back to Properties** and then click **Done**

10. Preview the scene.

11. Click the Play hotspot icon to play the audio.

12. Click the Stop hotspot icon to stop the audio.

13. Return to Edit mode.

Guided Activity 16: Control Object Visibility

1. Ensure that the **AudioGroupConditionMe** scenario is open.

2. Preview the **Aisle A** scene.

   There's a play audio icon and a stop audio icon.

3. Return to Edit mode.

4. Make an object initially invisible to learners.

   ☐ still working on the **Aisle A** scene, from the list of scene assets below the scene, select **Stop Audio**

   ☐ click the **Edit** icon

   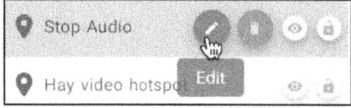

   The Hotspot options open.

   ☐ in the **Visible** area, click the slider to disable the option

   ☐ click the **Done** button

5. Preview the scene.

   There's a play audio icon but no stop audio icon.

Module 3: Audio, Groups, and Conditional Actions > Audio > Control Object Visibility

6. Return to Edit mode.

7. Add an action to an object that hides itself *and* shows another object.

    ☐ still working on the **Aisle A** scene, from the list of scene assets at the left, select **Play Aisle A Audio**

    ☐ click the **Edit** icon

    The Hotspot options reopen.

    ☐ click **Actions**

    ☐ working on the **On Select** tab, click the **Add Action** button

    ☐ click **Choose An Action**

    ☐ from the **Object Actions** area, click **Hide**

    ☐ from the **Objects** drop-down menu, select **This Object**

    ☐ click the **Add Action** button

    ☐ click **Choose An Action**

    ☐ from the **Object Actions** area, click **Show**

    ☐ from the **Objects** drop-down menu, select **Stop Audio**

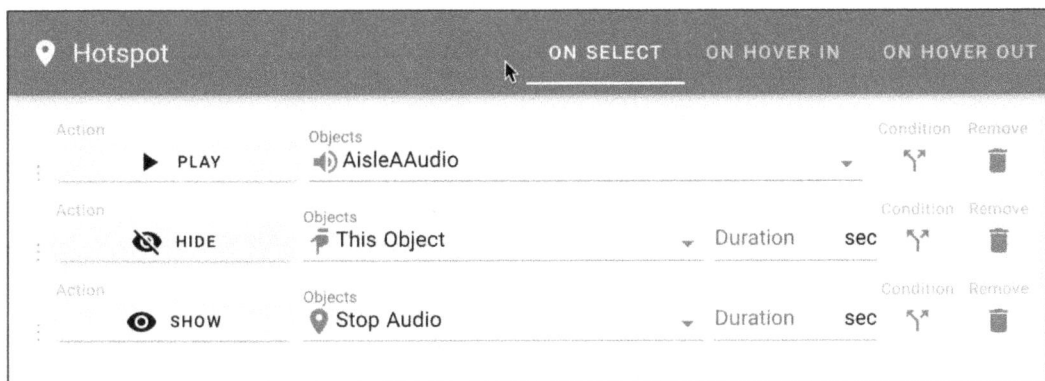

    ☐ click **Back to Properties** and then click **Done**

8. Preview the scene.

    Notice that the Stop audio icon is not visible.

9. Click the audio icon to play the audio.

    The audio plays, the audio icon disappears, and the stop icon appears onscreen.

10. Click the Stop icon to stop the audio.

11. Return to Edit mode.

Object Visibility Confidence Check

1. Edit the **Stop Audio** object.

2. Add two new actions: one that will hide "this object," and another that shows the **Play Aisle A Audio** object.

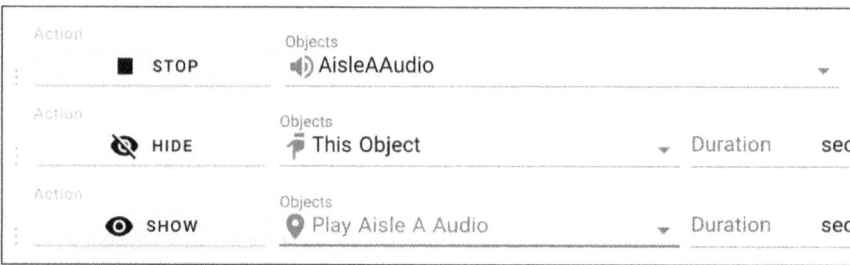

3. On the Canvas, drag the **Stop Audio** object on top of the **Audio** object.

4. Preview the scene.

5. Click the **audio** icon to hear the voiceover audio.

   Notice that once you click, the audio icon disappears and the stop audio icon takes its place.

6. Click the **stop** audio icon.

   The audio stops, the icon disappears, and is replaced by the audio icon.

7. Return to **Edit** mode.

8. Edit the **Show info about Kiki** object.

9. Add two actions: one that shows the **Kiki Information** and one that shows the **Close Kiki info hotspot**.

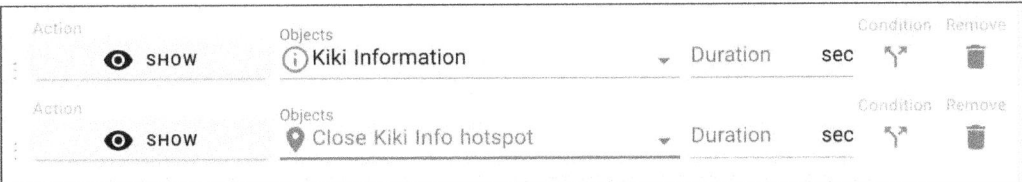

10. Edit the **Close Kiki info hotspot** object.
11. Add two actions: one that hides itself and the **Kiki Information**.

12. Preview the scene.
13. Click the hotspot target next to the cat.

    Information about the cat and a close icon appear.

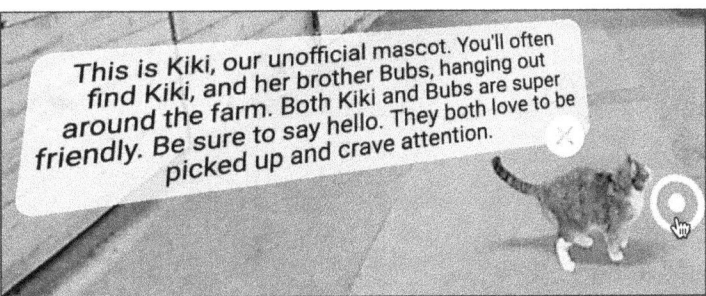

14. Click the close icon to hide the cat information and the close icon.
15. Return to Edit mode.

Grouping

There is no limit to how many objects you can add to any one scene. As you add more complex interactivity to a scene, such as drag and drop or quiz questions, you will need more scene objects. And you will likely need to create actions for those objects that interact with other scene objects.

If you group objects together, you'll find it easier to work with multiple scene objects and create actions for groups instead of individual objects.

In the activities that follow, you'll add three related objects to a scene and group them. Later, a conditional action will be used for the grouped objects.

Guided Activity 17: Add an Info Card and Image Hotspots

1. Ensure that you are in the **AudioGroupConditionMe** scenario.

2. If necessary, open the **Aisle A** scene.

3. Drag the canvas until you can see the barn door.

4. Add an Info Card.

   ☐ click the **Add Object** icon
   ☐ click **Add Info Card**

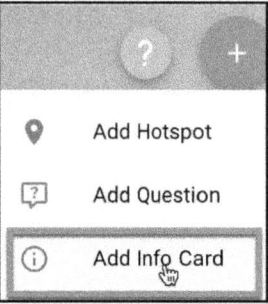

The Info Card options open.

Module 3: Audio, Groups, and Conditional Actions > Grouping > Add an Info Card and Image Hotspots

- [ ] name the Info Card **So soon text**
- [ ] type the following into the Info Card Text area: **Leaving so soon? You haven't visited everything just yet. Might we suggest that you continue the tour?**

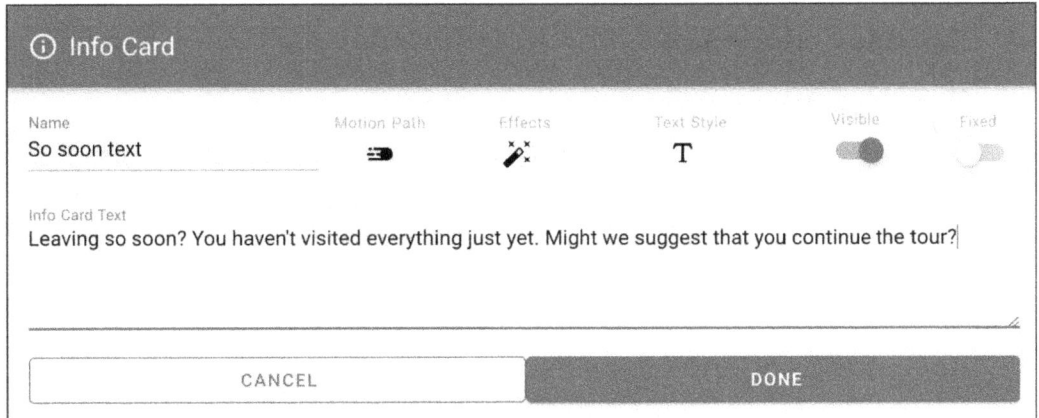

- [ ] click the **Done** button

5. Add an image hotspot.

   - [ ] click the **Add Object** icon
   - [ ] click **Add Hotspot**

   The Hotspot options open.

   - [ ] click the **Upload** icon
   - [ ] from **CVRData** > **images and videos**, open **ExitBarnButton.png**
   - [ ] rename the image slightly to **Exit Barn Button**

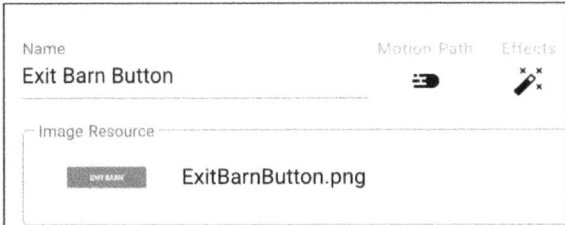

- [ ] click the **Done** button

6. Add another image hotspot.

   ☐ click the **Add Object** icon
   ☐ click **Add Hotspot**

   The Hotspot options open.

   ☐ click the **Upload** icon
   ☐ from **CVRData** > **images and videos**, open **ContinueTourButton.png**
   ☐ rename the image slightly to **Continue Tour Button**

   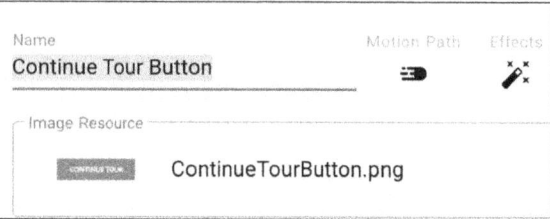

   ☐ click the **Done** button

7. Position the button images similar to what is shown in the image below.

Module 3: Audio, Groups, and Conditional Actions > Grouping > Group Objects

Guided Activity 18: Group Objects

1. Ensure that you are in the **AudioGroupConditionMe** scenario.

2. Ensure that you're in the **Aisle A** scene and that you can see the Info Card and button images you just added.

3. Select and group objects.

    ☐ select the **Info Card**

    ☐ press [ctrl] and click the **Exit Barn** button

    ☐ with the [ctrl] key still pressed, click the **Continue Tour** button

    The Info Card, Exit Barn button, and Continue Tour button should all be selected.

    ☐ right-click the selected objects and choose **Add to Group**

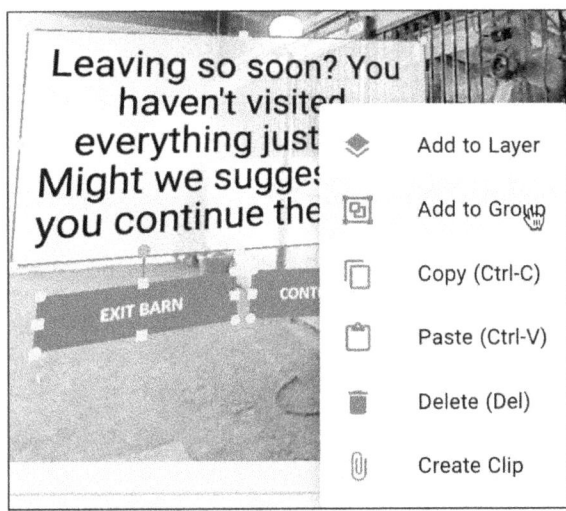

The new group appears among the scene objects list at the left. On the Canvas, grouped objects appear in a grid when selected.

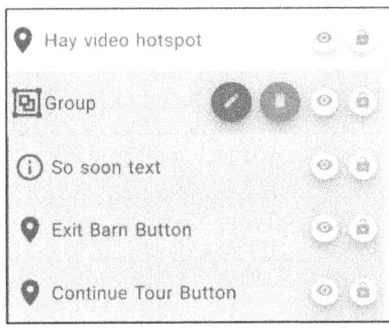 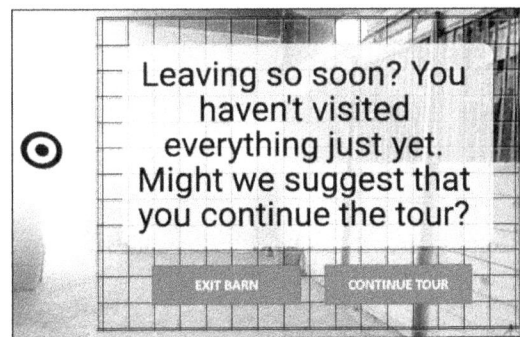

4. Edit a group.

   ☐ from the list at the left, **select** the **Group** and then click the **Edit** icon

   ☐ change the name to **So soon?**
   ☐ from the **Visible** area, click the slider to disable the option

   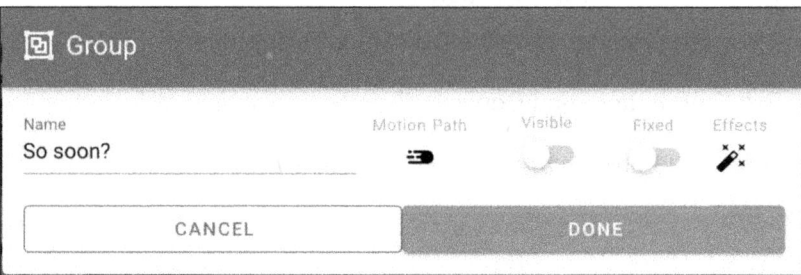

   ☐ click the **Done** button

Conditional Actions

As you have learned, you can assign one or more actions to an object that triggers when the learner selects, hovers over, or moves away from something. But you can also assign an action that only triggers under certain circumstances. For example, you can use conditional actions to prevent a learner from completing the course until after they have visited every scene in the project or clicked every hotspot.

Another great use of conditional actions is to prevent an action from triggering unless certain circumstances are true. Earlier in this book, you learned how to use the pan feature to elegantly move your learner from one part of a scene to another (see page 33). While panning is cool, you were cautioned that the panning feature isn't recommended if your learner is using a headset. You can create a conditional action that automatically prevents panning dependent upon the learner's hardware. If the learner is using a headset, panning is disabled.

Guided Activity 19: Create IF/AND Conditions

1. Ensure that you are in the **AudioGroupConditionMe** scenario.

2. Ensure that you're in the **Aisle A** scene.

3. Create a Conditional IF action that allows a learner to go to a scene only if a specific scene has been visited.

   ☐ from the list of scene objects at the left, select the **Back to the parking lot** hotspot
   ☐ click the **Edit** icon
   ☐ click **Actions**
   ☐ ensure that the **On Select** tab is active

   The object already has a simple action that links to the Parking Lot scene. The action is currently unconditional.

   ☐ click **Condition**

   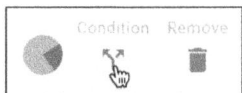

   An IF condition is added.

   ☐ from the **Object/Variable** drop-down menu, choose **Tack Room**
   ☐ from the **Condition** drop-down menu, choose **Has Been Visited**

   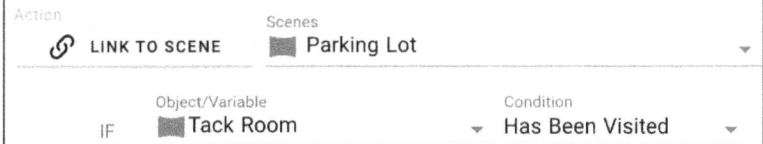

4. Add an AND Condition.

   ☐ click **Condition**

   A second line is added to the Action—AND. Conditional lines can be set to AND or OR. You can toggle between the options by clicking the word AND.

   ☐ ensure that the condition is set to **AND**

   ☐ from the **Object/Variable** drop-down menu, choose **Visitor Room**

   ☐ from the **Condition** drop-down menu, choose **Has Been Visited**

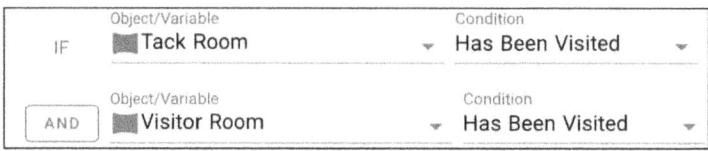

5. Add a third Condition.

   ☐ click **Condition**

   A third AND line is added to the condition.

   ☐ from the **Object/Variable** drop-down menu, choose **Indoor Arena**

   ☐ from the **Condition** drop-down menu, choose **Has Been Visited**

6. Add a fourth Condition.

   ☐ click **Condition**

   A fourth AND line is added to the condition.

   ☐ from the **Object/Variable** drop-down menu, choose **Aisle B**

   ☐ from the **Condition** drop-down menu, choose **Has Been Visited**

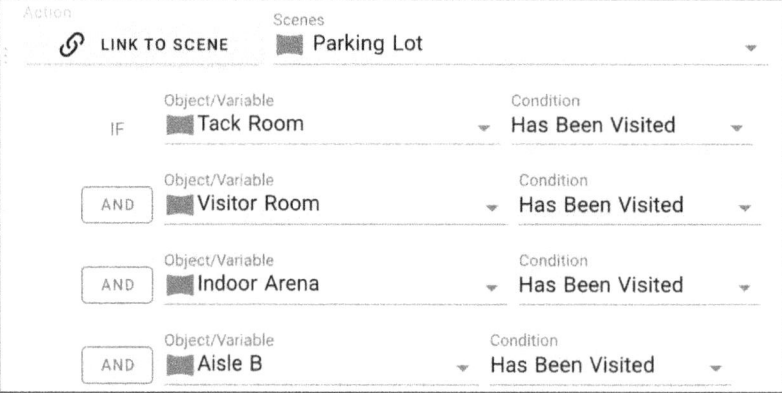

7. Add a final AND Condition.

   ☐ click **Condition**

   ☐ from the **Object/Variable** drop-down menu, choose **Aisle A**

   ☐ from the **Condition** drop-down menu, choose **Has Been Visited**

Thanks to the conditions, the hotspot to the parking lot will not work unless the learner has visited *all* of the listed scenes. However, learners won't get any feedback as to why the hotspot isn't working. Next, you'll add a conditional action that displays the **So Soon?** group if the required scenes have not been visited.

Leave the Hotspot properties open for the next activity.

Guided Activity 20: Create IF/OR Conditions

1. Ensure that the hotspot properties for the **Back to the parking lot** hotspot are still open.

2. Add an Action that will show the "So soon?" group.

    ☐ click **Add Action**

    ☐ click **Choose an Action**

    ☐ from the **Object Actions** area, choose **Show**

    ☐ from the **Objects** drop-down menu, choose the **So soon?** group

3. Make the Action conditional.

    ☐ click **Condition**

    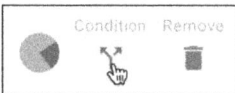

    An IF condition is added.

    ☐ from the **Object/Variable** drop-down menu, choose **Tack Room**

    ☐ from the **Condition** drop-down menu, choose **Has Not Been Visited**

4. Add an OR Condition.

    ☐ click **Condition**

    ☐ click the word **AND** to change it to **OR**

    ☐ from the **Object/Variable** drop-down menu, choose **Visitor Room**

    ☐ from the **Condition** drop-down menu, choose **Has Not Been Visited**

    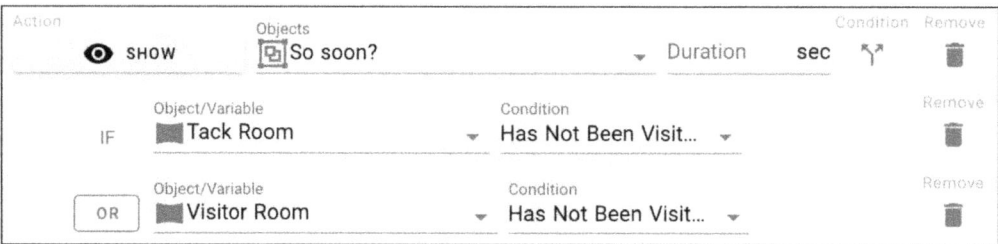

Conditional Actions Confidence Check

1. Add **3 more** Conditions to the action that will only show the **So soon?** group if the Indoor Arena, Aisle B, and Aisle A **have not been visited**.

   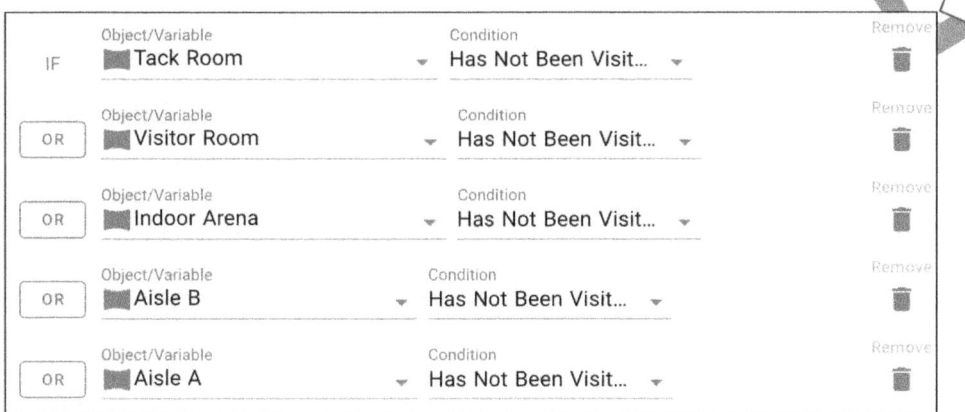

2. Click **Back to Properties**
3. click **Done**.
4. Select the **Barn Entrance scene**.
5. Preview the scene.
6. Enter the main barn entrance to get to **Aisle A**.

   At this point, you have not visited any of the required scenes except for Aisle A.

7. Turn and click the barn door hotspot to leave the barn.
8. The **So soon?** group (the text and the two buttons) appears. Neither the Exit Barn or Continue Tour buttons are currently working so there is no need to click them.
9. Exit the preview.
10. In the **So Soon?** group, add an action to the **Exit Barn** button that links to the Parking Lot scene.

    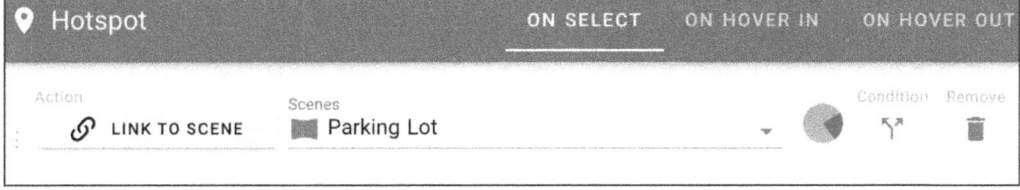

11. In the **So soon?** group, add two actions to the **Continue Tour** button.

    One action that links to the Aisle A scene.

    One action that Hides the **So soon?** group.

    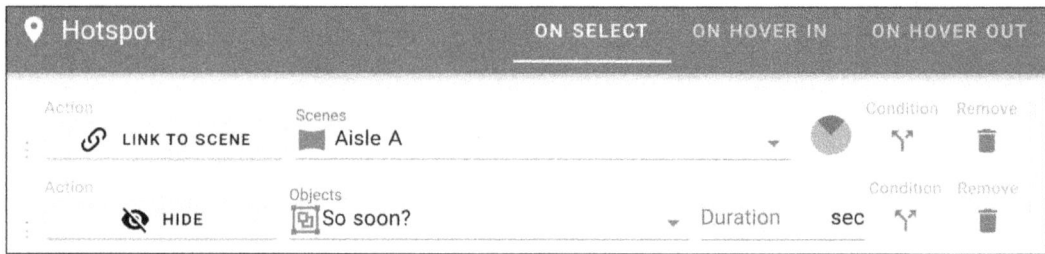

12. Preview the scene again and test the buttons in the **So soon?** group.
13. Exit the preview.
14. Open the **Barn Entrance** scene.
15. Edit the **Welcome audio** object.
16. Disable the **Autoplay** feature.

    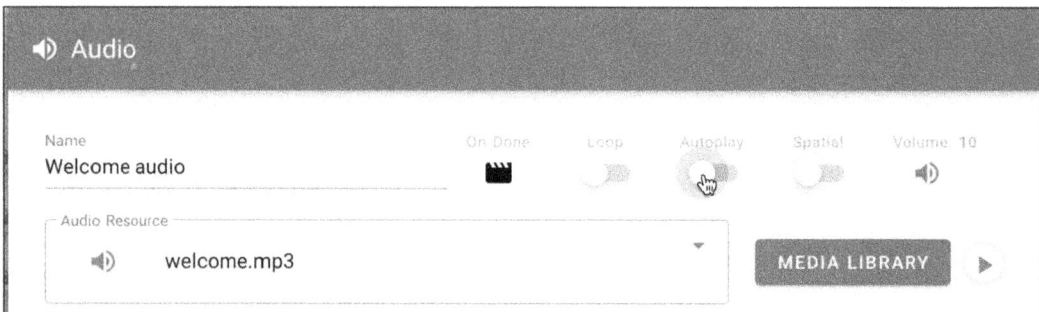

17. Edit the **Barn Entrance** scene.

18. Click **On Show**.

19. Add a conditional action that plays the Welcome audio only if it has not been played already.

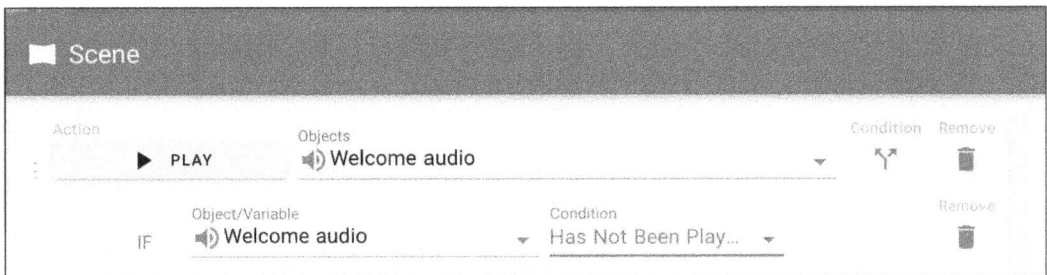

20. Open the **Parking Lot** scene.
21. Edit the **Thanks audio** object.
22. Disable the **Autoplay** feature.
23. Edit the **Parking Lot** scene.
24. Click **On Show**.
25. Add a conditional action that plays the **Thanks audio** only if it has not been played already.

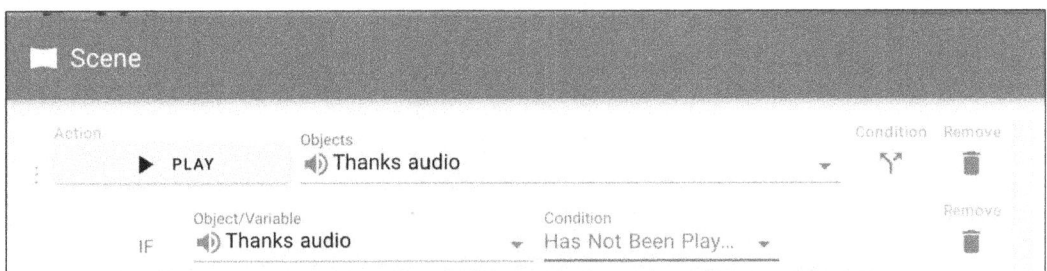

26. Open the **Barn Entrance** scene.
27. Preview the scene and enter the **small door** at the left of the barn.
28. Immediately turn and exit the barn to return to the parking lot.

    You'll hear the "Thanks" audio.

29. Turn and re-enter the barn using the small door.
30. Immediately turn and exit the barn again.

    Because you have already heard the "Thanks" audio, it does not play again.

31. Exit the preview.

When you were introduced to the concept of conditional actions, one use-case was to prevent panning if the user was on the VR platform (using a VR headset). Let's set up that conditional scenario now.

32. On the **Barn Entrance**, scene, insert an **Info Card** using the information shown below. Note that the card should not be visible initially.

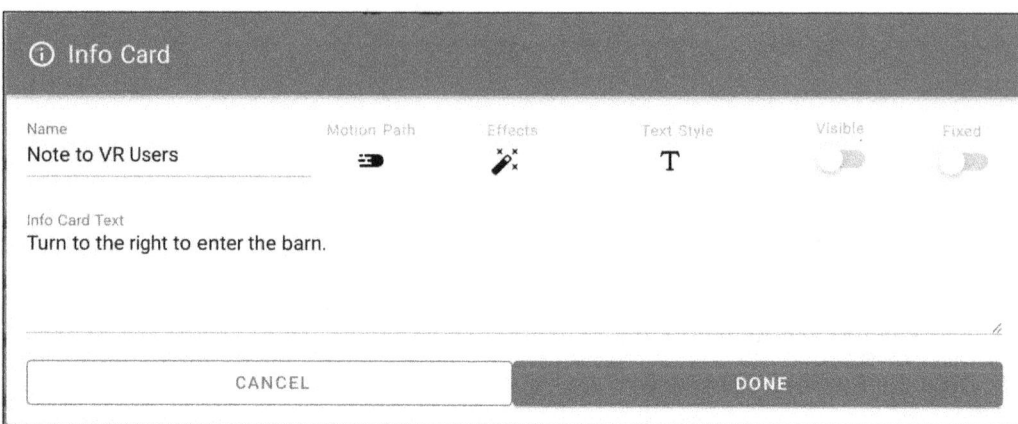

33. On the **Barn Entrance**, scene, edit the **Start Button**.

34. Using the image below as your guide, add a condition to the **Pan to** action *and* add a conditional **Show** action. Note that the IF statement is going to be Platform specific, VR users.

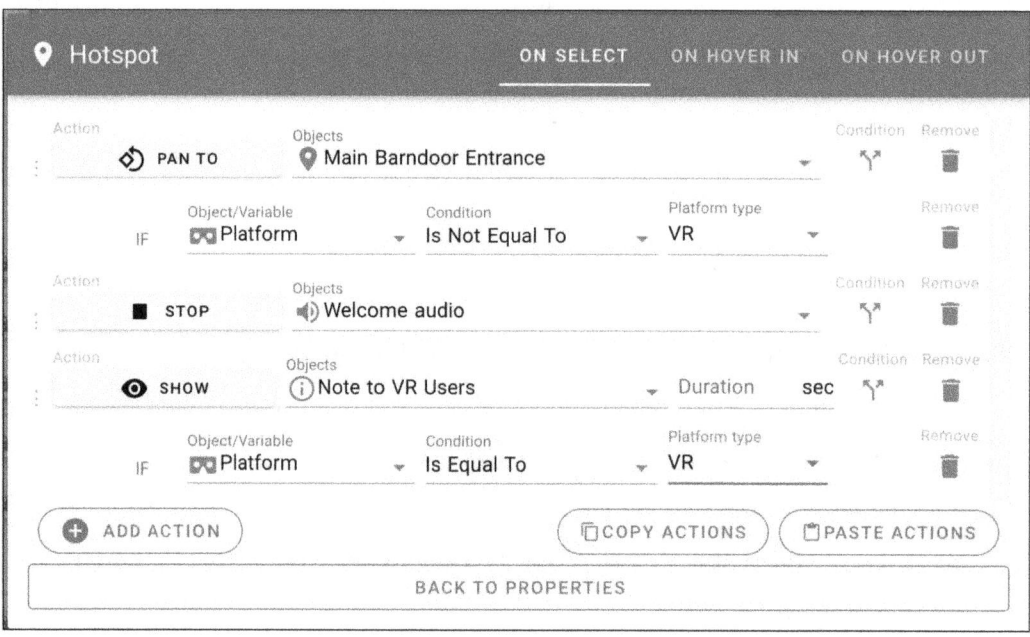

Unless you have a VR headset, there is no way to test this final conditional action.

35. When finished, click the Cenario VR logo to return to My Scenarios.

"Skills and Drills" Learning

Module 4: Layers, Drag and Drop, and Timed Events

In This Module You Will Learn About:

- Layers, page 64
- Drag and Drop, page 68
- Timed Events, page 74
- Motion Paths, page 78

And You Will Learn To:

- Create a Layer, page 64
- Make an Object a Drop Spot, page 68
- Make an Object a Drag Item, page 69
- Add a "Reset" Action, page 72
- Insert an Action Object, page 74
- Add Timed Events, page 75
- Create and Edit a Motion Path, page 78

Layers

You learned about groups on page 50. Groups and layers are both used to organize canvas objects. If you need to control the alignment of objects or have multiple objects move together, you would use a group. if you want to keep objects together but don't need them to have a relationship to each other, you would use a layer.

Guided Activity 21: Create a Layer

1. Ensure that you are logged into CenarioVR and on the **My Scenarios** screen.

2. Import the **LayerMeDragMe.zip** project from **CVRData > scenarios**.

3. Open the **LayerMeDragMe** scenario.

4. Open the **Indoor Arena** scene.

5. Create a layer.

    ☐ from the list of objects on the left, select **Which Saddle**

    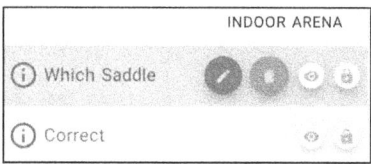

    On the Canvas, the "Sam is coming to the barn..." Info Card is selected.

    ☐ press [**shift**] on your keyboard and, from the list of objects on the left, select **Western Saddle**

    ☐ release [**shift**]

    Seven objects should be selected.

    ☐ right-click the selected objects and choose **Add to Layer**

    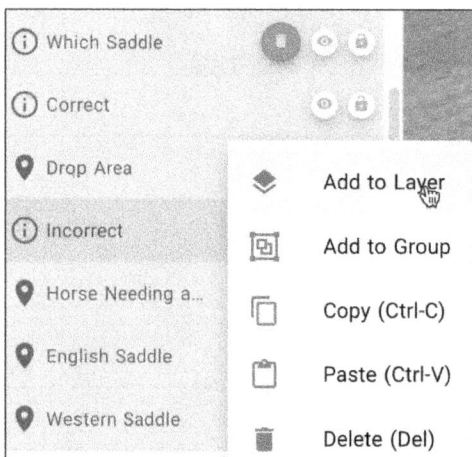

    An untitled layer appears in the object list with the default name "Layer." The layer contains all of the selected objects.

Note: Objects can be easily added or removed from a layer by dragging. You can also right-click a layer object and choose **Remove from layer**.

6. Rename a layer.

    ☐ on the list of objects, click the word **Layer** and then click the **Edit** icon

    The Layer properties open.

    ☐ change the layer's name to **Drag and Drop Challenge Layer**

    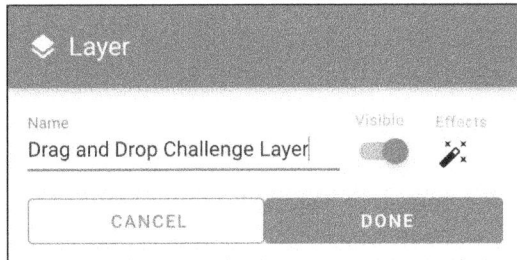

    ☐ click the **Done** button

7. Make all of the objects in a layer invisible to the learner by default.

    ☐ on the list of objects, click **Drag and Drop Challenge Layer**

    ☐ click the **Edit** icon

    ☐ click the **Visible** slider 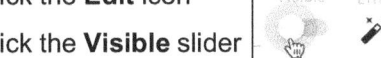 to disable the feature

    ☐ click the **Done** button

    The Visible option does not hide the layer or its objects on the Canvas. The Visible option actually hides the layer objects from the learner, which you can confirm by previewing.

8. Switch to Preview mode and confirm that all of the objects in the layer are hidden. (Besides the arena, the only thing you should see if the light bulb icon.)

9. Return to Edit mode.

10. Add an action to show a layer.

    ☐ on the **Canvas**, double-click the **light bulb** to open the Hotspot properties

    ☐ click **Actions**

    ☐ with the **On Select** tab selected, click **Add Action**

    ☐ click **Choose An Action**

    ☐ from the **Object Actions** area, click **Show**

    ☐ from the **Objects** drop-down menu, choose **Drag and Drop Challenge Layer**

11. Add an action that forces an object to hide itself.

    ☐ with the **Hotspot** options for the **light bulb icon** still open and with the **On Select** tab selected, click **Add Action**

    ☐ click **Choose An Action**

    ☐ from the **Object Actions** area, click **Hide**

    ☐ from the **Objects** drop-down menu, choose **This Object**

    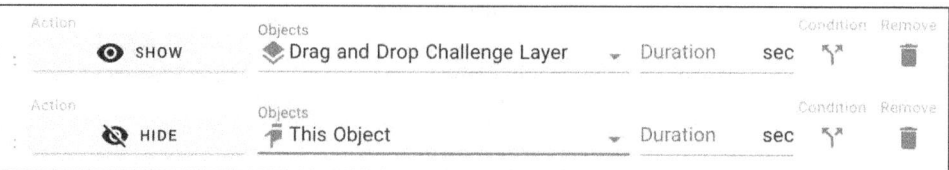

12. Add an action that hides the correct and incorrect text.

    ☐ with the **On Select** tab selected, click **Add Action**

    ☐ click **Choose An Action**

    ☐ from the **Object Actions** area, click **Hide**

    ☐ from the **Objects** drop-down menu, choose **Correct**

    ☐ click **Add Action**

    ☐ click **Choose An Action**

    ☐ from the **Object Actions** area, click **Hide**

    ☐ from the **Objects** drop-down menu, choose **Incorrect**

    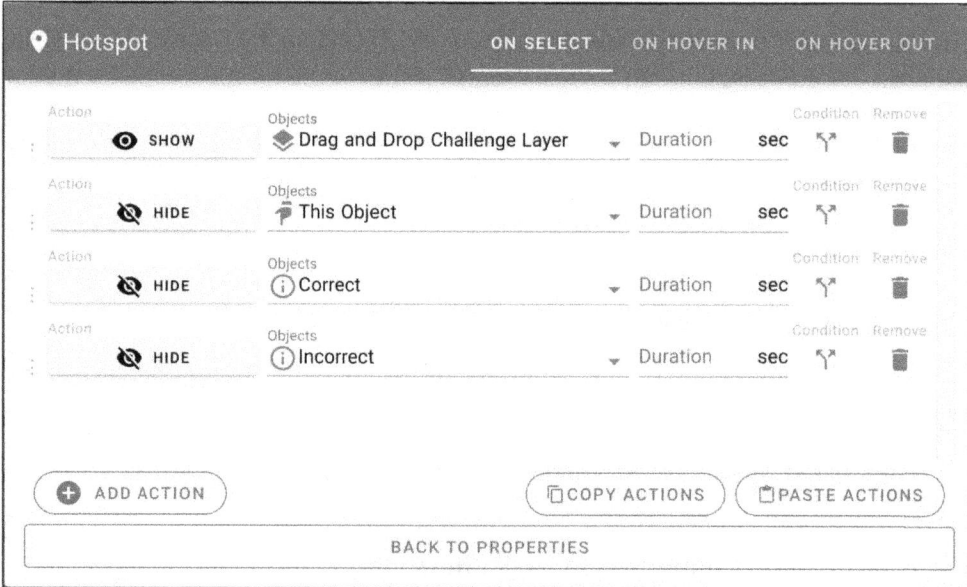

    ☐ click **Back to Properties**

    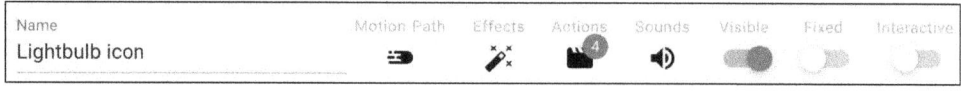

    ☐ click **Done**

13. Switch to Preview mode.

    At first, only the light bulb icon appears onscreen.

14. Click the light bulb icon.

    The layer and its objects appear except for the two feedback Info Cards. Also notice that after having been clicked, the light bulb icon hides itself.

15. Return to Edit mode.

Drag and Drop

Few things fully engage the learner more than interactivity. And allowing learners to move things around the screen—dragging and dropping—is at, or near, the top of the list when it comes to including meaningful interactivity in your eLearning project.

During activities in this section, you will learn how to create a drag and drop interaction that allows learners to drag one of two saddles to a target. If the learner drags the correct saddle to the target, they'll see a "correct" message; otherwise they'll see an "incorrect" message.

Guided Activity 22: Make an Object a Drop Spot

1. Ensure that you are in the **LayerMeDragMe** scenario.

2. Ensure that you are in the **Indoor Arena** scene.

3. Specify an object as a drop area.

   ☐ from the list of objects in the **Drag and Drop Challenge Layer** at the left, select **Drop Area**

   This object is simply a transparent hotspot on the back of the horse. You learned how to add a transparent hotspot beginning on page 31.

   ☐ double-click the Drop Area hotspot

   The Hotspot options open.

   ☐ from the upper right of the window, click the **Interactive** slider to enable the option

   ☐ from the **Interactive Type** drop-down menu, choose **Drop Spot - Single Object**

   ☐ click the **Done** button

Module 4: Layers, Drag and Drop, and Timed Events > Drag and Drop > Make an Object a Drag Item

Guided Activity 23: Make an Object a Drag Item

1. Ensure that you are in the **LayerMeDragMe** scenario.

2. Ensure that you are in the **Indoor Arena** scene.

3. Specify an object as a drag item.

    ☐ from the list of objects in the **Drag and Drop Challenge Layer** at the left, select and edit the **English Saddle**

    ☐ from the upper right of the Hotspot window, enable **Interactive**

    ☐ from the **Interactive Type** drop-down menu, choose **Drag Item**

    ☐ click the **Done** button

4. Preview the scene.

5. Click the light bulb icon to display the **Drag and Drop Challenge** layer.

6. Drag the English saddle—the saddle on the right—to the horse.

    After dropping the saddle on the horse, there's no feedback letting you know if the correct saddle was dragged (it wasn't). In addition, there isn't currently a way to drag the Western saddle to the horse. You'll fix both issues during the Confidence Check that follows.

7. Return to Edit mode.

© 2024, IconLogic, Inc. All Rights Reserved. 69

Drag and Drop Confidence Check

1. Ensure that you are in the **LayerMeDragMe** scenario.
2. Ensure that you are in the **Indoor Arena** scene.
3. Edit the **English** saddle.
4. Add an **Action** that **Shows** the **Incorrect** object **On Drop**.

5. Make the Western saddle an interactive Drag Item.

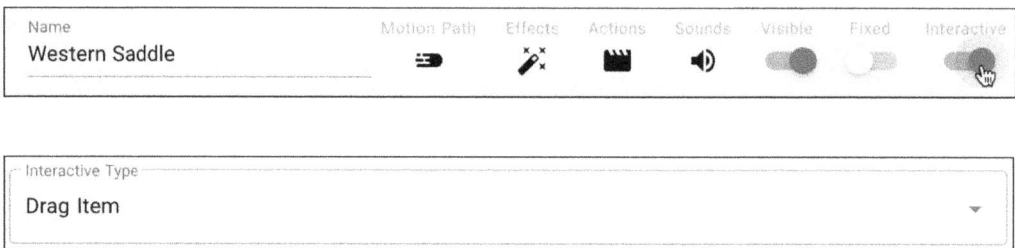

6. Add an **Action** to the Western saddle **Shows** the **Correct** object **On Drop**.

7. Preview the scene.
8. Click the light bulb icon to display the layer.
9. Drag the English saddle to the horse.

   Because the English saddle is not the correct saddle for riding Western, the incorrect message appears.

10. Drag the other saddle to the horse.

   Things work, sort of. When the Western saddle is dropped onto the horse, the correct message appears. However, the incorrect message is also on-screen. *And* the Western saddle snaps back to its original position. You'll learn how to use a reset action to fix this issue next.

11. Return to Edit mode.

Guided Activity 24: Add a "Reset" Action

1. Ensure that you are in the **LayerMeDragMe** scenario, within the **Indoor Arena** scene.

2. Add a Reset action to the English saddle.

    ☐ on the Canvas, double-click the **English** saddle (reminder: the English saddle is the saddle on the right)

    The Hotspot options appear.

    ☐ click **Actions**
    ☐ click **Add Action**
    ☐ click **Choose An Action**
    ☐ from the **Object Actions** area, click **Reset**
    ☐ from the **Objects** drop-down menu, choose **This Object**

    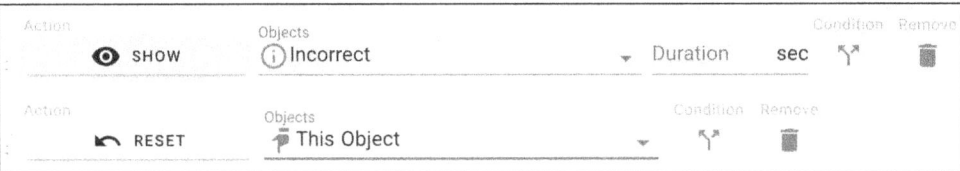

    ☐ click **Back to Properties**
    ☐ click **Done**

3. Add Hide and Reset actions to the Western saddle.

    ☐ on the Canvas, double-click the **Western** saddle

    The Hotspot options appear.

    ☐ click **Actions**
    ☐ click **Add Action**
    ☐ click **Choose An Action**
    ☐ from the **Object Actions** area, click **Reset**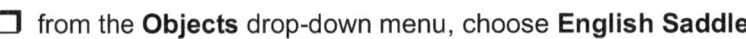
    ☐ from the **Objects** drop-down menu, choose **English Saddle**
    ☐ click **Add Action**
    ☐ click **Choose An Action**
    ☐ from the **Object Actions** area, click **Hide**
    ☐ from the **Objects** drop-down menu, choose **Incorrect**
    ☐ click **Back to Properties**
    ☐ click **Done**

4. Preview the scene.

5. Click the light bulb icon to display the layer.

6. Drag the **English** saddle onto the horse.

   After dropping the English saddle onto the horse, the incorrect feedback message appears *and* the saddle returns to its original canvas position.

7. Drag the **Western** saddle to the horse.

   The correct message appears *and* the incorrect message disappears.

8. Return to Edit mode.

CenarioVR: The Essentials (Second Edition)

Timed Events

You can add objects and/or animations to a scene that triggers at a specific time. For instance, on the Indoor Arena scene, the entire drag and drop interaction that you created is predicated upon the learner clicking the light bulb icon. If the icon isn't clicked, the learner won't know that there's an interaction.

One approach to the problem is to insert an Info Card onto the scene instructing learners to click the light bulb. But an Info Card could clutter the scene. Many of your learners will click the light bulb icon out of simple curiosity. For those learners who arrive in the arena and either don't recognize the light bulb as interactive or don't think to click it, you can add an event that highlights the light bulb icon if it hasn't been clicked within a specific amount of time. Of course, you can make the action conditional so that the highlight won't occur if the light bulb is clicked.

Guided Activity 25: Insert an Action Object

1. Ensure that you are in the **LayerMeDragMe** scenario, within the **Indoor Arena** scene.

2. Insert an Action Object.

    ☐ click the **arrow** at the right of the CenarioVR window to expand the assets panel

    ☐ click the **Actions** tab

    ☐ double-click **Arrow Left** to add the image to the Canvas

3. Move and resize the arrow image similar to the image below.

4. Name the image and set its initial state to hidden.

    ☐ double-click the arrow image to open the Hotspot properties

    ☐ name the arrow **Interaction prompt arrow**

    ☐ click the **Visible** slider to disable the option

    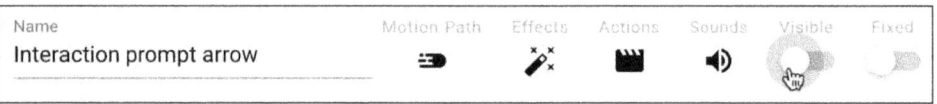

    ☐ click the **Done** button

Module 4: Layers, Drag and Drop, and Timed Events > Timed Events > Add Timed Events

Guided Activity 26: Add Timed Events

1. Ensure that you are in the **LayerMeDragMe** scenario, within the **Indoor Arena** scene.

2. Add a timed event.

    ❏ at the bottom of the window, click the **Add Event at current time** icon

    The Timed Events screen opens.

    ❏ name the event **Arrow prompt appears**

    ❏ change the seconds to **10**

3. Choose an action for the timed event.

    ❏ from the **Action** area, click **Choose an Action**

    ❏ from the **Object Actions** area, click **Show** 👁

    ❏ from the **Objects** drop-down menu, choose **Interaction prompt arrow**

    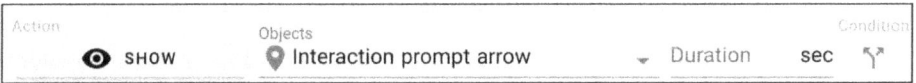

4. Make the action conditional.

    ❏ click **Condition**

    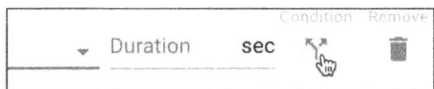

    ❏ click the **IF Object/Variable** drop-down menu

    ❏ choose **Lightbulb icon**

    ❏ change the **Condition** to **Has Not Been Selected**

    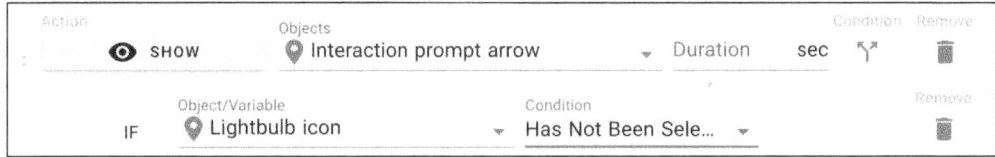

    ❏ click the **Done** button

Notice the position of the red flag on the timeline. This is a visual indicator of the timed event that you just added.

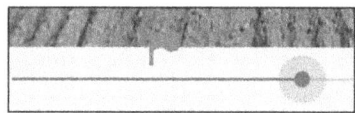

5. Preview the scene.

   Provided that you do not click the light bulb icon, after 10 seconds the arrow appears onscreen.

6. Return to Edit mode.

7. Preview the scene again.

8. Click the light bulb icon to display the layer.

   Because you clicked the light bulb, the arrow does not appear.

9. Return to Edit mode.

Timed Actions Confidence Check

1. Ensure that you are in the **LayerMeDragMe** scenario.
2. Ensure that you are in the **Indoor Arena** scene.
3. Add a second timed event to the **Timeline** named **Arrow Spins**.
4. Set the Timed Event to occur at **12** seconds.

5. Add the **Spin X Axis animation** action to the **Interaction prompt arrow**.
6. Limit the Spin X Axis animation to **2 spins**.

7. Preview the scene.
8. After 10 seconds, the arrow appears on-screen.
9. After a few more seconds, the arrow attempts to further get your attention by spinning.
10. Return to Edit mode.

Motion Paths

Beyond simply animating an object, you can create a motion path and have any object follow that path as it appears on-screen. During the activity that follows, you'll create a motion path for the Interaction prompt arrow.

Guided Activity 27: Create and Edit a Motion Path

1. Ensure that you are in the **LayerMeDragMe** scenario.

2. Ensure that you are in the **Indoor Arena** scene.

   You're about to add a motion path animation to the interaction prompt arrow. There's already an animation applied to the object. It isn't necessary to add both a motion path and an animation to an object. Let's remove the animation event.

3. Remove a timed event.

   ☐ on the **Timeline**, double-click the Arrow spins event you added at 12-seconds

   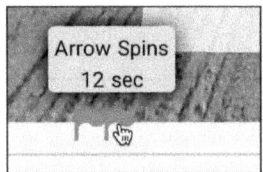

   The Timed Event screen opens.

   ☐ click **Remove Event**

4. Create a motion path.

   ☐ on the Canvas, double-click the **interaction prompt arrow**

   The Hotspot options open.

   ☐ click **Motion Path**

   The Create New Motion Path screen opens. You've already set up a Timed Event for the arrow to appear on-screen after 10 seconds. The Motion Path Start Time needs to match that timing.

   ☐ change the Start Time to **10**

   ☐ click the **Create** button

   You are prompted to create the motion path. Your first motion is the most important. This establishes where the arrow is positioned when the motion path begins.

Module 4: Layers, Drag and Drop, and Timed Events > Motion Paths > Create and Edit a Motion Path

☐ on the Canvas, drag the arrow a few inches to the right

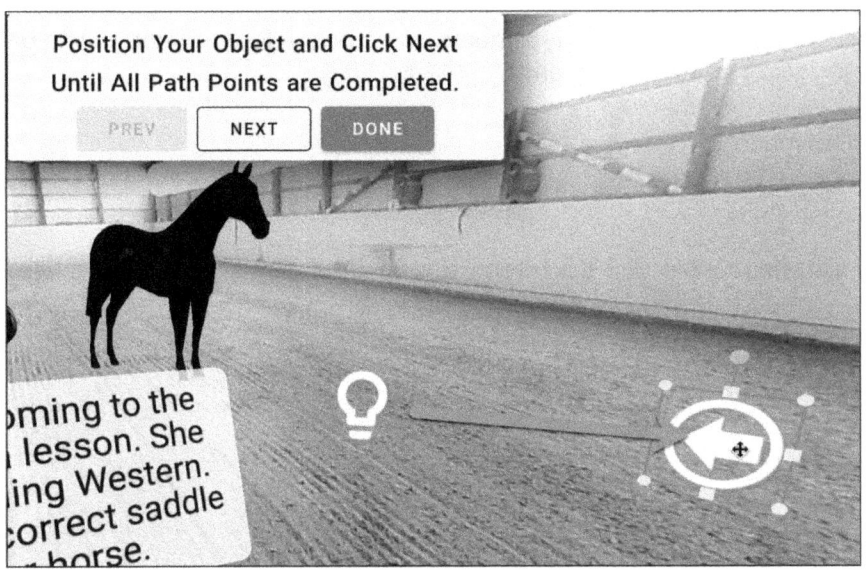

☐ click the **Next** button
☐ drag the arrow up a bit and about half way toward the light bulb

The dotted line you see as you drag the arrow is the motion path.

☐ click the **Next** button
☐ drag the arrow close to the light bulb *and* drag the green circle above the arrow to rotate it a bit toward the light bulb

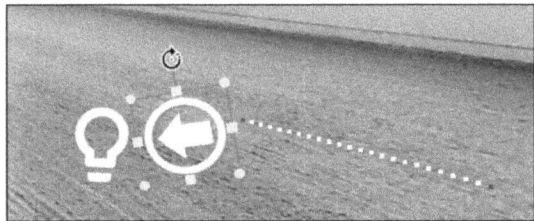

☐ click **Done**
☐ click **Back to Properties**

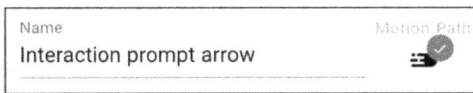

☐ click **Done**

5. Preview the scene.

6. After 10 seconds, the arrow not only appears on-screen, it follows your motion path (including the slight rotation at the end)

7. Return to Edit mode.

8. Edit the Motion Path.

    ☐ on the Canvas, double-click the **interaction prompt arrow**

    The Hotspot options reopen.

    ☐ click **Motion Path**

    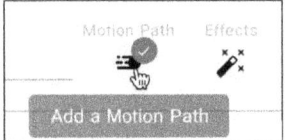

    ☐ click **Edit Path**

    ☐ on the Canvas, move the arrow up a bit
    ☐ click **Next**
    ☐ on the Canvas, move the arrow up or down a bit
    ☐ click **Done**
    ☐ click **Back to Properties**
    ☐ click **Done**

9. Preview the scene.

10. After 10 seconds, the arrow arrives onscreen and follows the edited motion path.

11. Return to Edit mode.

"Skills and Drills" Learning

Module 5: Quizzes and Variables

In This Module You Will Learn About:

- Quizzes, page 82
- Variables, page 92

And You Will Learn To:

- Add a Quiz Question, page 82
- Set Up Quiz Question Feedback, page 87
- Use a Variable to Display Quiz Results, page 92
- Create Custom Variables, page 97
- Add a "Modify Variable" Action, page 98

Quizzes

Learning can be exhausting. As a professional trainer, I learned long ago that there's only so much learning that can effectively occur over a set amount of time. I can force-feed information to my students over multiple hours and days. However, without regularly scheduled breaks and ample opportunity to practice, the ability of students to both learn and retain information is minimized.

Beyond time to practice and regularly scheduled breaks, I also encourage my learners to openly discuss what they are learning in class, during class. I've found that classroom discussions and real-world anecdotes enhance understanding of the concepts and improve information retention rates. When it comes to eLearning, there isn't a live trainer and there aren't any classmates. How is a learner supposed to share the knowledge gained during an eLearning course when there isn't an opportunity for live discussion? One solution is to add a quiz to the course. In addition to measuring the effectiveness of the course content, as they answer the quiz questions, students are forced to think about what they learned.

During the activities that follow, you will learn how to add quiz questions to a scenario. Later, you'll learn how variables allow you to both track quiz scores and display quiz results to the learner.

Guided Activity 28: Add a Quiz Question

1. Ensure that you are logged into CenarioVR and on the **My Scenarios** screen.

2. Import the **QuizMe.zip** project from **CVRData > scenarios**.

3. Open the **QuizMe** scenario.

4. Open the **Tack Room** scene.

   There are two interactive objects in the room along with several hidden objects. At the left, notice that there is a hotspot. The hotspot has already been set up to show information about the Western saddle. At the right, there is another hotspot that has already been set up to show information about English saddle

5. Review some of the object actions.

   ☐ from the list of scene objects at the left, **edit** the **English Saddle hotspot** to open the Hotspot properties

   ☐ click **Actions**

   When clicked by the learner, the hotspot will show information about the English saddle, play supporting audio, display a close icon, *and* display a checkmark. You've learned how to create these types of actions during previous activities.

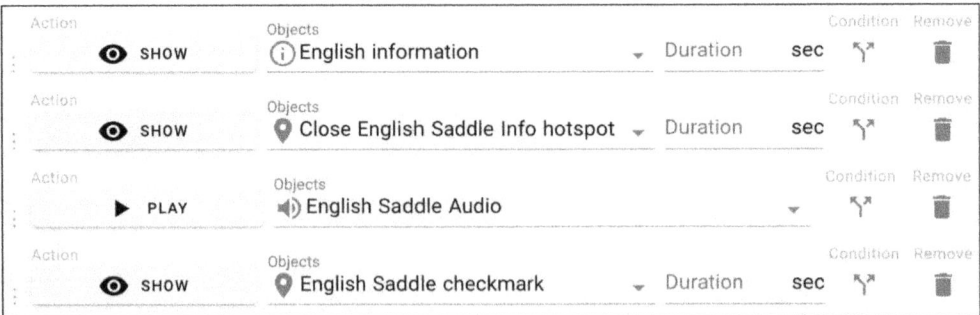

Module 5: Quizzes and Variables > Quizzes > Add a Quiz Question

- ☐ click **Back to Properties**
- ☐ click **Cancel**
- ☐ from the list of scene objects at the left, **edit** the **Close English Saddle Info** hotspot to open the Hotspot properties
- ☐ click **Actions**

Beyond closing itself when clicked, the **Close English Saddle Info** hotspot hides the **English information** and immediately **stops the audio**. Notice that there is an incomplete **Show** action that you will complete later. First, you're going to create a quiz question about the English saddle. The question will be hidden to learners by default. Once you are finished creating the quiz question, you will return here and complete the conditional action so that the quiz question shows only if the question hasn't already been answered.

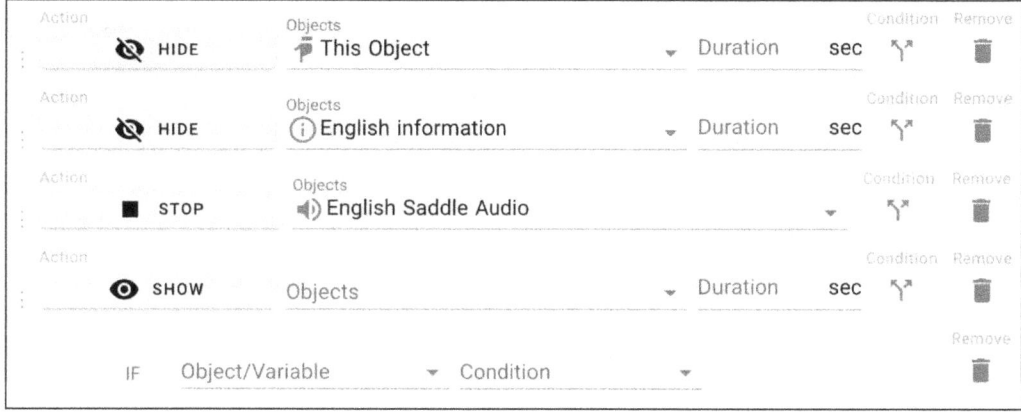

- ☐ click **Back to Properties**
- ☐ click **Cancel**

6. Add a quiz question, rename it, and disable its visibility.

   - ☐ deselect anything within the group

   A moment ago, you were viewing information for an object within the **English saddle group**. If a group is selected, new objects are automatically added to the group. You can always right-click an object and remove it from a group, but by deselecting the group prior to adding the quiz question, you'll ensure that the object you are about to add won't be added to the group.

   - ☐ click the **Add Object** icon and choose **Add Question**

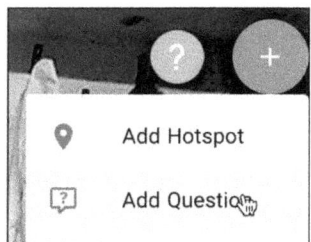

The Question options open.

- ☐ name the question **English Question**
- ☐ click the **Visible** slider to **disable** the option
- ☐ click the **Hide On Answer** slider to disable the option

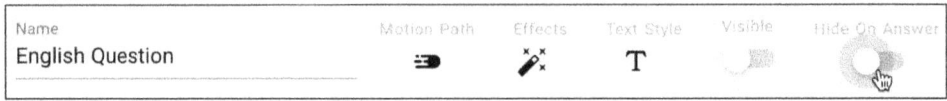

7. Add question text.

   ☐ type the following into the **Question Text** area: **A general term that encompasses any type of forward seat riding.**

8. Select an appearance for the quiz question.

   ☐ from the **Appearance** drop-down menu, choose **Question Card, lettered choices**

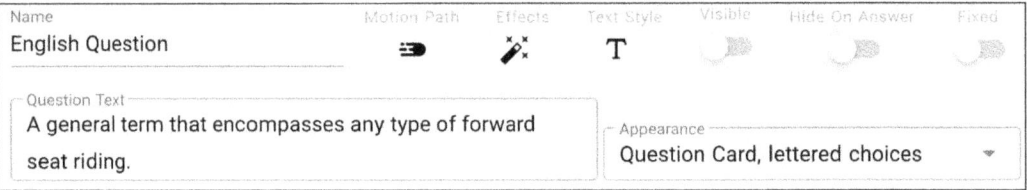

9. Edit and add answer choices.
   - ☐ change **Choice Text A** to **Hunt Seat**
   - ☐ change **Choice Text B** to **Dressage**
   - ☐ click **Add Choice**
   - ☐ change **Choice Text C** to **Western pleasure**
   - ☐ click **Add Choice**
   - ☐ change **Choice Text D** to **Horsemanship**

	Choice Text
A	Hunt Seat
B	Dressage
C	Western pleasure
D	Horsemanship

10. Specify a correct answer.
    - ☐ to the right of **Answer A, Hunt Seat**, click the slider for **Correct** to enable **Answer A** as the correct choice

    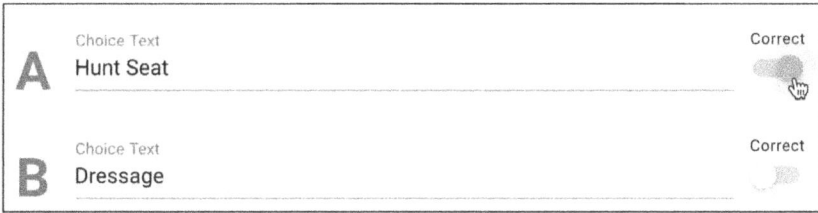

    - ☐ click the **Done** button

11. Drag the quiz question and position it on the back wall of the room similar to what is shown in the image below.

    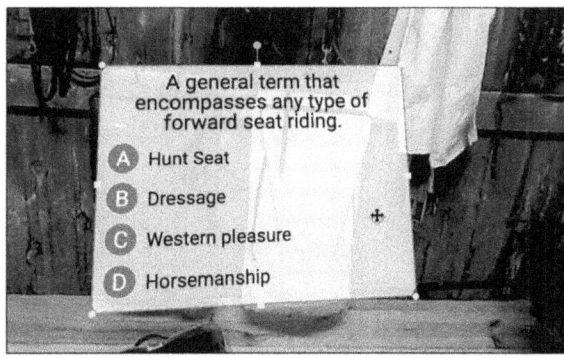

12. Preview the scene.

13. Scroll to the right and click the hotspot on the English saddle.

    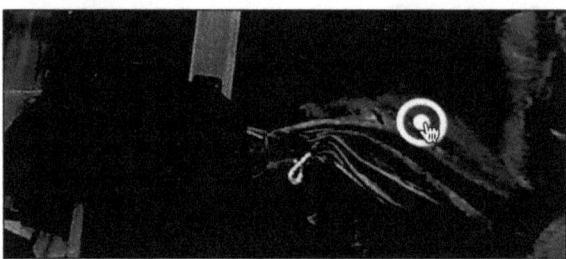

    Information about the saddle opens.

14. Click the close icon to close the information about the English saddle.

    Clicking the close icon should not only close the information about the saddle, it should display the quiz question. However, as you learned when you started this activity, the necessary action is not set up.

15. Return to Edit mode.

16. Edit an action.

    ☐ from the list of scene objects at the left, edit the **Close English Saddle Info** hotspot to open the Hotspot properties

    ☐ click **Actions**

    ☐ from the **Show** action area, click the **Objects** drop-down menu, scroll down, and then choose **English Question**

    ☐ in the **IF** condition, click the **Object/Variable** drop-down menu and, from the Tack Room scene, choose **English Question**

    ☐ ensure that the **Condition** is set to **Has Not Been Answered**

    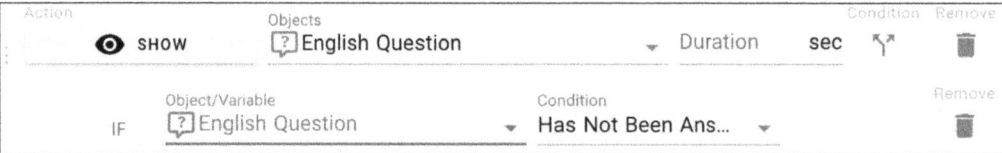

    ☐ click **Back to Properties** and then click **Done**

17. Preview the scene.

18. Click the hotspot at the right of the scene (the hotspot on the English saddle) and then click the close icon to close the information about the English saddle.

    This time, the quiz question appears.

19. Click any of the answers to attempt to answer the question.

    Unfortunately, it doesn't matter how you answer the question because there isn't any feedback. No worries, you'll tackle that issue next.

20. Return to Edit mode.

Module 5: Quizzes and Variables > Quizzes > Set Up Quiz Question Feedback

Guided Activity 29: Set Up Quiz Question Feedback

1. Ensure that you are in the **QuizMe** scenario.

2. Ensure that you are working in the **Tack Room** scene.

3. Review the hidden quiz question correct and incorrect feedback.

   ☐ from the list of scene objects at the left, notice two groups: **English Question Correct Answer** and **English Question Incorrect Response**.

   Both groups are currently hidden from view on the Canvas. Because this scene has multiple objects, the ability to hide and show scene objects is a nice feature that minimizes screen clutter.

   ☐ to the right of the **English Question Correct Answer** group, click **Edit Mode Visibility**

   The correct answer feedback appears onscreen.

   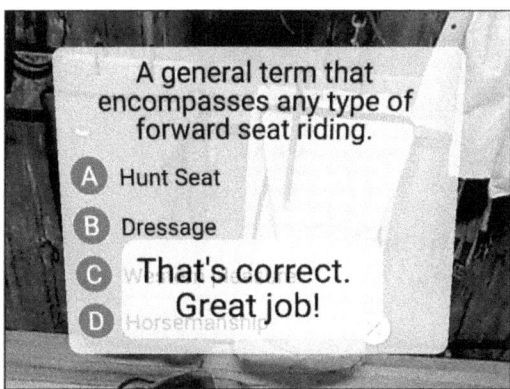

4. Attach the English Question Correct Answer group as the English Question correct answer.

   ☐ from the list of scene objects at the left, edit the **English Question**.

   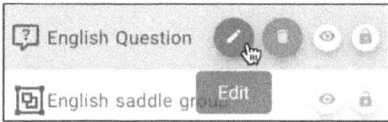

   The Question options open.

   ☐ confirm that **Hunt Seat** is set as the **correct** answer

   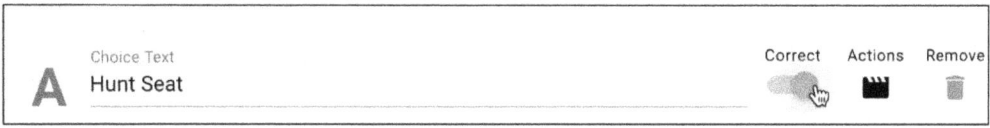

- [ ] to the right of A) Hunt Seat, click **Actions**
- [ ] click **Choose An Action**
- [ ] from the **Object Actions** area, click **Show**
- [ ] click the **Objects** drop-down menu and choose **English Question Correct Answer group**

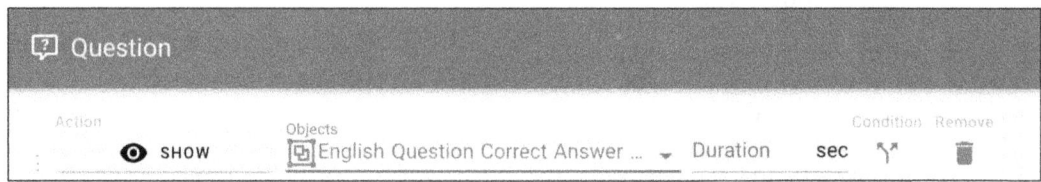

- [ ] click **Back to Question**

- [ ] click **Done**

5. Preview the scene.

6. Click the hotspot at the right of the scene (the hotspot on the English saddle).

7. Click the close icon to close the information about the English saddle.

   The quiz question appears.

8. Answer the question correctly by clicking **Hunt Seat**.

   The "Correct" feedback appears.

9. Return to Edit mode.

Module 5: Quizzes and Variables > Quizzes > Set Up Quiz Question Feedback

Quiz Question Confidence Check

1. Edit the **English Question** and add an action to each of the incorrect choices that shows the **English Question Incorrect Response Group**.

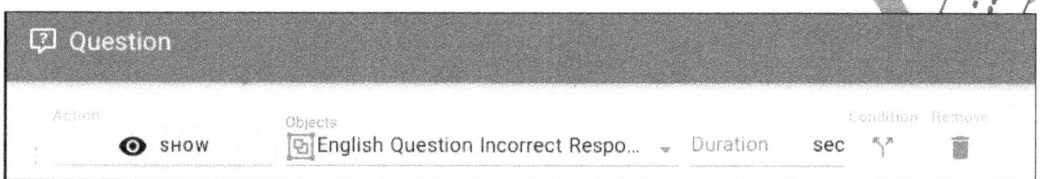

   Note: You can make quick work out of adding actions to other objects by using the **Copy Actions** and **Paste Actions** features.

2. Preview the scene.
3. Click the hotspot at the right of the scene (the hotspot on the English saddle).
4. Click the close icon to close the information about the English saddle.
5. The quiz question reappears.
6. Answer the question incorrectly by clicking anything other than **Hunt Seat**.
7. The "Incorrect" feedback appears.
8. Return to Edit mode.
9. Add a new question named **Western Question** using the images below as your guide (Note that **Visible** and **Hide on Answer** are both **disabled**.)

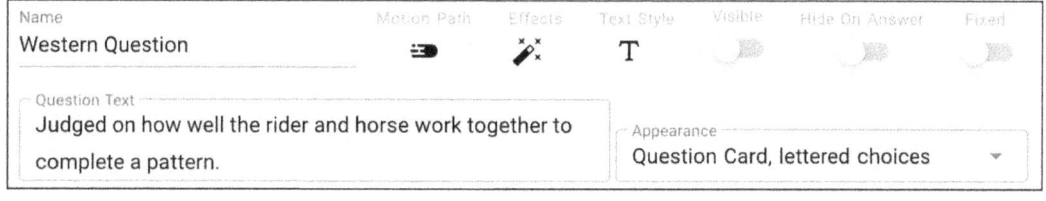

10. Add the following choices (note that Choice Text D, Horsemanship, is the correct answer).

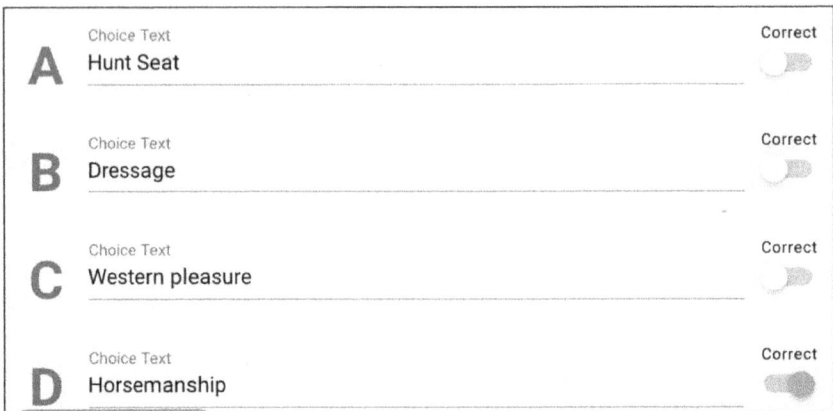

11. Add an **Action** to choice **D** that shows **Western Question Correct Response Group**.

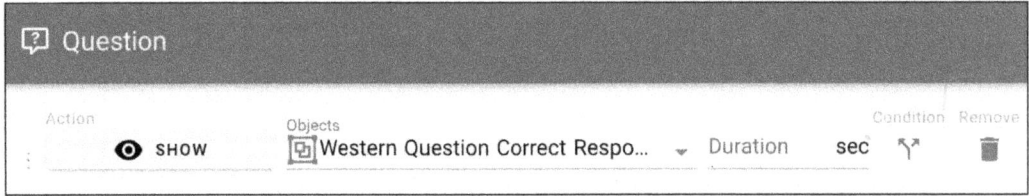

12. Add an **Action** to the other three choices that shows **Western Question Incorrect Response Group**.

    Note: If the Canvas is getting cluttered again, use the **Edit Mode Visibility** option to hide or show objects and/or groups on the Canvas.

13. Edit the actions for the **Close Western Saddle Info hotspot** object so that the **Western Question shows** *if* the question has not been answered already.

    Note: There is an incomplete **Pan To action** for both the **Close Western Saddle Info** and **Close English Saddle Info** hotspots. If you'd like, you can complete those actions as shown in the image below. However, if the actions remain incomplete, they will not negatively impact this activity.

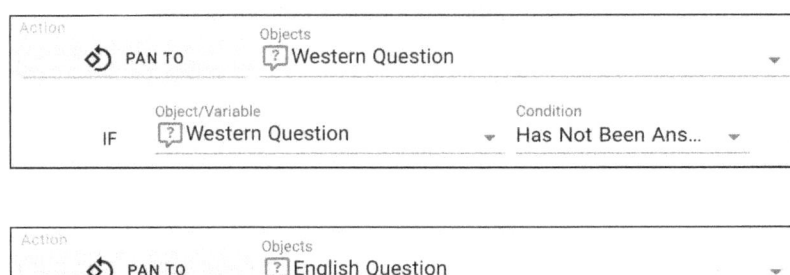

14. Edit the actions for the **Close English Correct** hotspot and, if necessary, ensure there is an Action to **Hide** the English Question.

15. Edit the actions for the **Close Western Correct** hotspot and, if necessary, ensure there is an Action to **Hide** the Western Question.

16. Preview the scene.

17. After reviewing information about each saddle, you should be able to answer both quiz questions.

18. Return to Edit mode.

Variables

Variables serve as buckets for data. The data can be used to provide feedback to the learner and/or allow you as the developer to create conditional scenarios. For instance, you could use a variable to capture the quiz score. Once a learner completes a quiz in your scenario, the quiz score can be displayed to the learner and reported to a Learning Management System (LMS).

By default, every scenario includes a variable called "SCORE," which automatically keeps track of a quiz score that is calculated based on the number of questions in a scenario. If there are four questions in a scenario, each question is worth 25 points. If there are ten questions, each question is worth 10 points.

You can also create your own variables. During the lessons that follow, you'll leverage the SCORE variable so learners will see how they did on the saddles quiz in the Tack Room. You'll also create variables that alert the learner if they haven't visited a specific scene in the course.

Guided Activity 30: Use a Variable to Display Quiz Results

1. Ensure that you are logged into CenarioVR and on the **My Scenarios** screen.

2. Import the **VariableMe.zip** project from **CVRData > scenarios**.

3. Open the **VariableMe** scenario.

4. Review the current project variables.

    ☐ click the **Scenario Settings and Publish** icon

    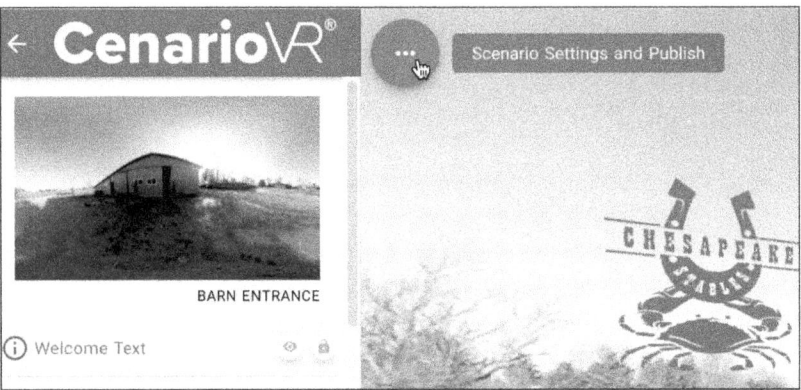

    ☐ click **Variables**

    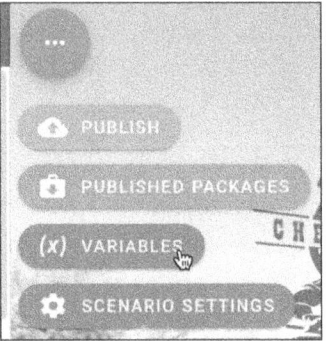

Module 5: Quizzes and Variables > Variables > Use a Variable to Display Quiz Results

The project variables appear. Notice that there are two default variables: SCORE and PLATFORM. You'll be referencing the SCORE variable in the Track Room scene in a moment. To reference the SCORE variable, you can type **%SCORE%** or **%score%**. The percent signs tell CenarioVR that you're referencing a variable. All will be well so long as the variable is spelled correctly. The typing isn't case sensitive, but watch for typos.

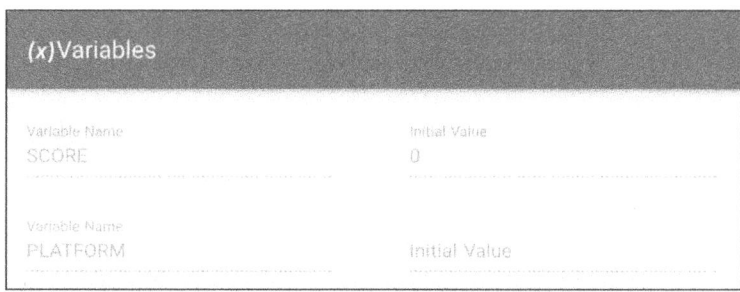

☐ click **Done**

5. Reference the SCORE variable in an Info Card.

☐ open the **Tack Room** scene

☐ from the list of objects at the left, **Quiz score group**, click **Edit Mode Visibility**

An Info Card and "reset" icon appear. The Info Card contains a placeholder you'll replace with a reference to the SCORE variable.

☐ on the **Canvas**, double-click the **Info Card** to open the Info Card options

☐ replace the phrase **<<Reference the SCORE variable here>>** with **%SCORE%**

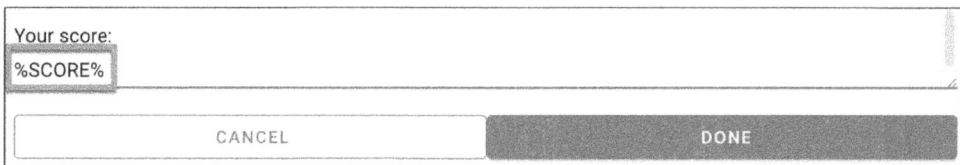

☐ click **Done**

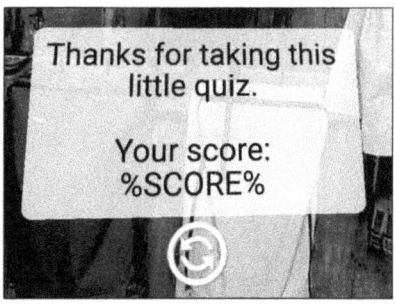

© 2024, IconLogic, Inc. All Rights Reserved.

6. Add a conditional action that will display the Quiz score group only if both quiz questions are answered.

   ☐ from the list of objects on the left, **English Question Correct Answers group**, edit the **Close English Correct** hotspot

   ☐ click **Actions**

   ☐ click **Add Action**

   ☐ click **Choose An Action**

   ☐ from the **Object Actions** area, click **Show**

   ☐ from the **Objects** drop-down menu, choose **Quiz score group**

   ☐ to the right of **Show > Quiz score group**, click **Condition**

   ☐ from the **IF Object/Variable** drop-down menu, choose **English Question**

   ☐ from the **Condition** drop-down menu, choose **Has Been Answered**

   ☐ to the right of **Show > Quiz score group**, click **Condition** again

   The word **AND** appears beneath the IF condition. This additional condition can be toggled to **OR** by clicking **AND**. You'll be leaving this as an AND condition.

   ☐ from the **Object/Variable** drop-down menu, choose **Western Question**

   ☐ from the **Condition** drop-down menu, choose **Has Been Answered**

   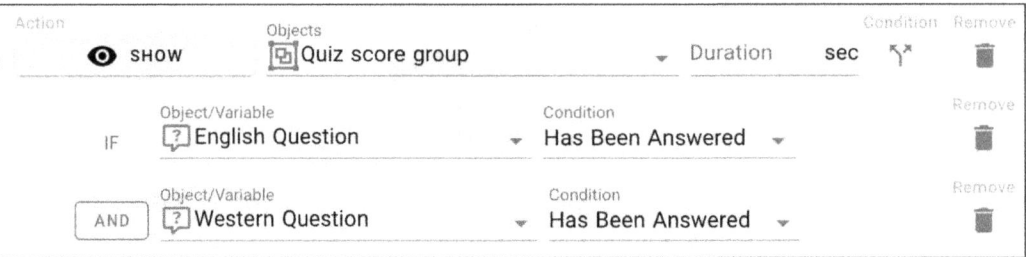

   ☐ click **Back to Properties**

   ☐ click **Done**

Module 5: Quizzes and Variables > Variables > Use a Variable to Display Quiz Results

Conditional Actions Confidence Check

1. Add the same conditional action that will Show the **Quiz score group** to the following scene objects:

   ☐ Close English Incorrect

   ☐ Close Western Correct

   ☐ Close Western Incorrect

   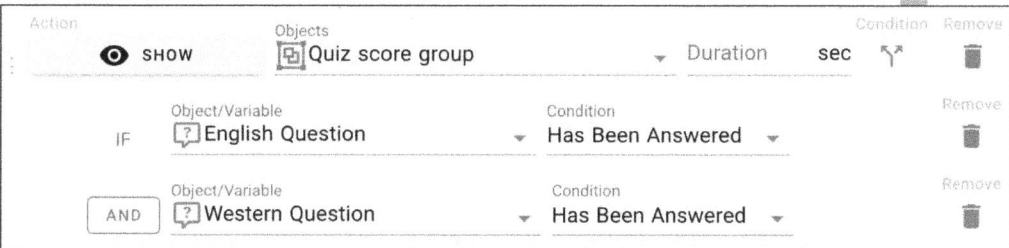

2. Preview the scene.

3. Take the quiz.

   Once you close the feedback for the second quiz question, the quiz score appears. As mentioned earlier, the points are split evenly across all quiz questions. Because you only have two questions, each question is worth 50 points. I missed one of the questions, hence my score of 50 as shown below.

   Notice also that there's a "Reset" icon below the quiz results. You'll get that working next. Once you've set it up, the "Reset" icon will allow the learner to retake the quiz.

   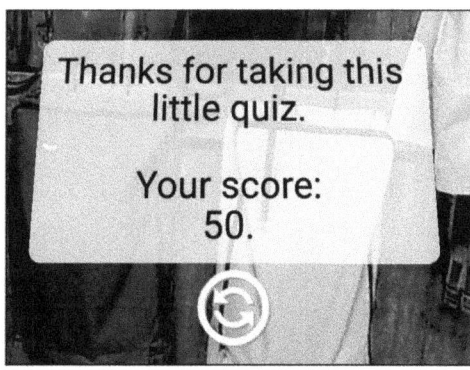

4. Return to **Edit** mode.

5. Edit the **Reset Quiz** icon.

6. Add two actions:
   - ☐ One action to **Hide** the **Quiz score group**
   - ☐ One action to **Reset** the **quiz**

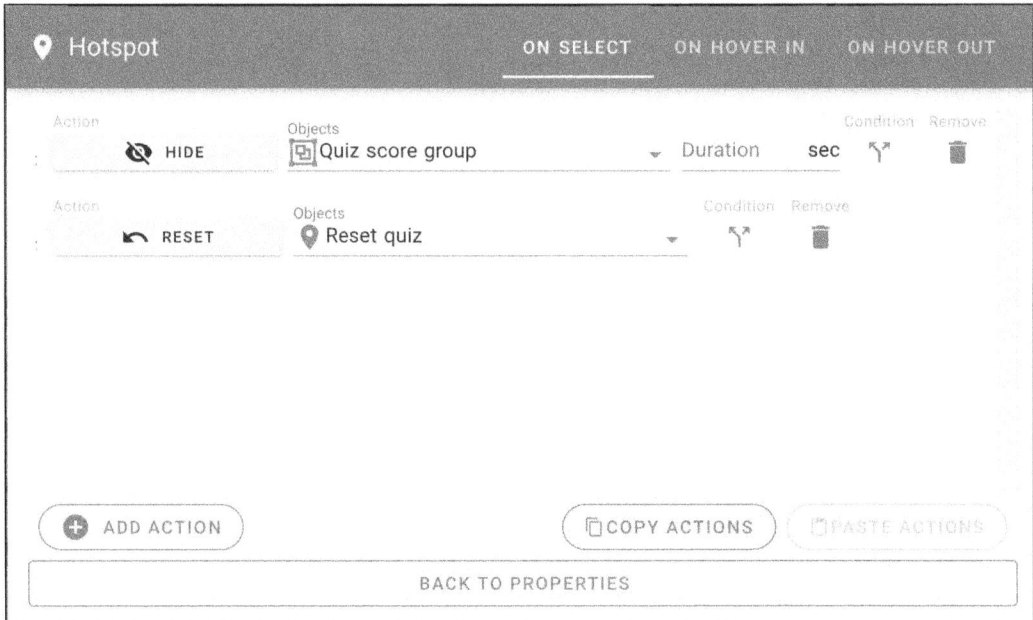

7. Preview the scene.
8. Take the quiz.
9. After the quiz score appears, click the **Reset** icon.

   The quiz score group disappears and the quiz is reset. You should now be able to take the quiz again if you'd like.

10. Return to **Edit** mode.

Guided Activity 31: Create Custom Variables

1. Ensure that the **VariableMe** scenario is open.

2. Add a Variable.

   ☐ click the **Scenario Settings and Publish** icon

   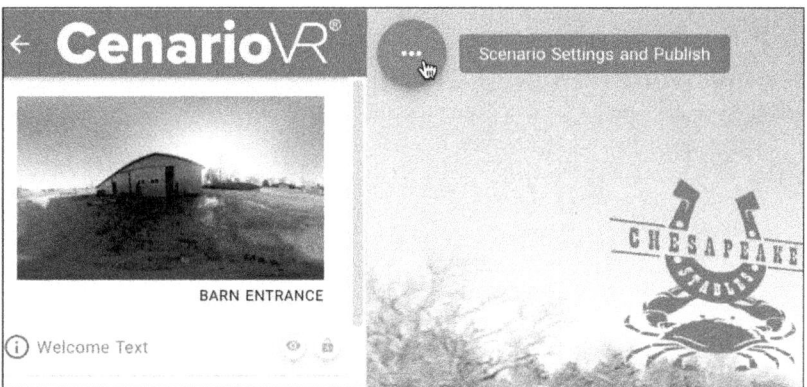

   ☐ click **Variables**

   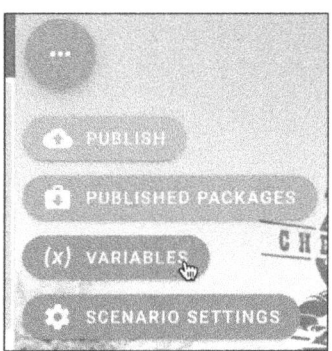

   The Variables options appear.

   ☐ click **Add Variable**
   ☐ name the variable **AisleA**
   ☐ in the **Initial Value** field, type **Not Visited**

   ☐ click **Done**

Guided Activity 32: Add a "Modify Variable" Action

1. Ensure that the **VariableMe** scenario is open.

2. Open the AisleA scene.

3. Add a Modify Variable action.

    ☐ from the top of the **AisleA** scene, click **Edit Scene Properties**

    ☐ click **On Show**
    ☐ click **Add Action**
    ☐ click **Choose an Action**
    ☐ from the **Variables, Completion and Automation** area, click **Modify Variable**
    ☐ from the **Name** drop-down menu, choose **AisleA**

    AisleA is the variable you created during the last activity.

    ☐ from the **Type** drop-down menu, choose **Set Variable Value**
    ☐ in the **Value** field, type **Visited**

    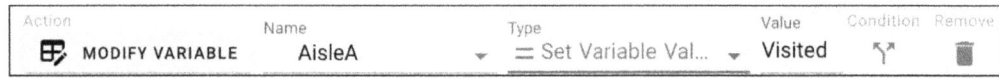

    ☐ click **Back to Properties**
    ☐ click **Done**

4. Reference the AisleA variable in an Info Card.

    ☐ in the **Aisle A** scene, edit the **So soon text** Info Card
    ☐ to the right of Aisle A: type **%AisleA%**

    ☐ click **Done**

Module 5: Quizzes and Variables > Variables > Add a "Modify Variable" Action

5. Test the variable.

    ☐ select the **Barn Entrance** scene
    ☐ preview the scene
    ☐ enter the main barn door
    ☐ turn and attempt to exit the barn door

    You'll be alerted that you have not yet visited all of the rooms. Aisle A shows as visited.

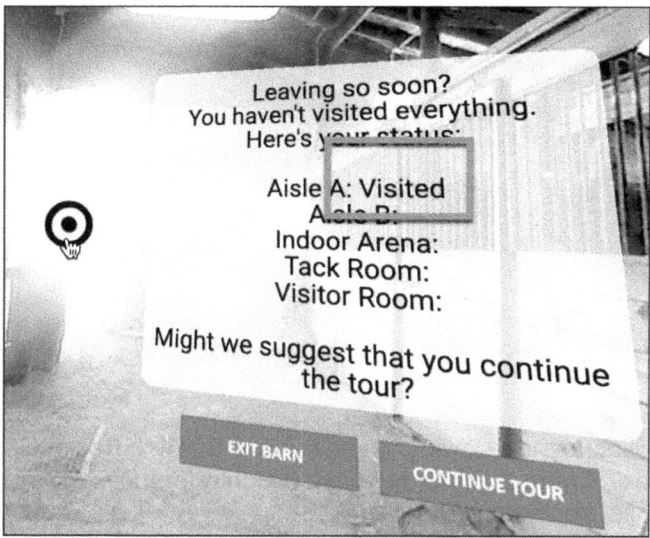

6. Return to Edit mode.

Custom Variables Confidence Check

1. Add the following variables to the project: **AisleB**, **Arena**, **TackRoom**, and **VisitorRoom**. Set the initial value for each to Not Visited.

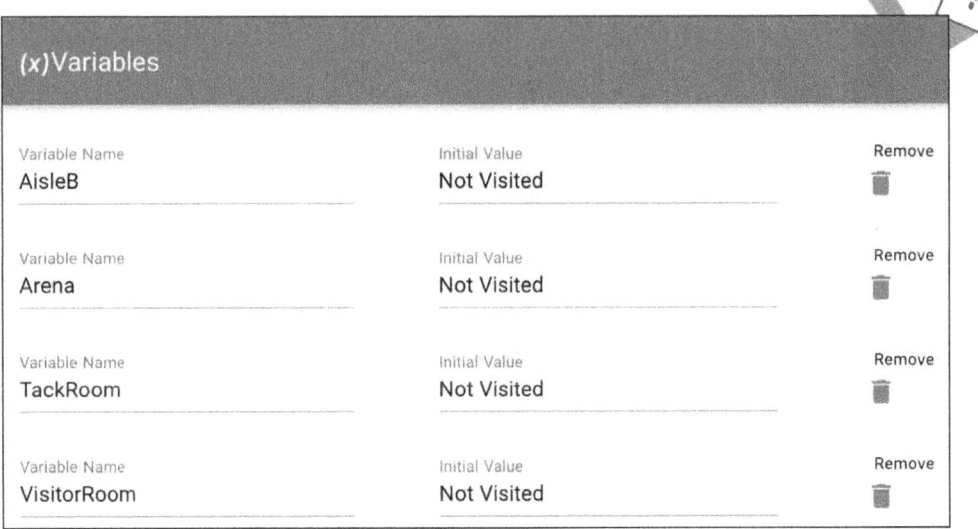

2. Add the **Modify Variable** action to the following scenes: **Aisle B**, **Tack Room**, **Visitor Room**, and the **Indoor Arena** (ensure that each action references the scene's variable as appropriate *and* set each value to Visited).

   The image below is the Modify Variable action for the Tack Room.

   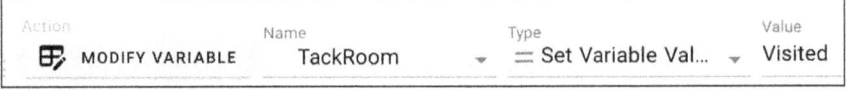

3. Reference each of the variables in the **So soon text** Info Cards in Aisle A and Aisle B.

   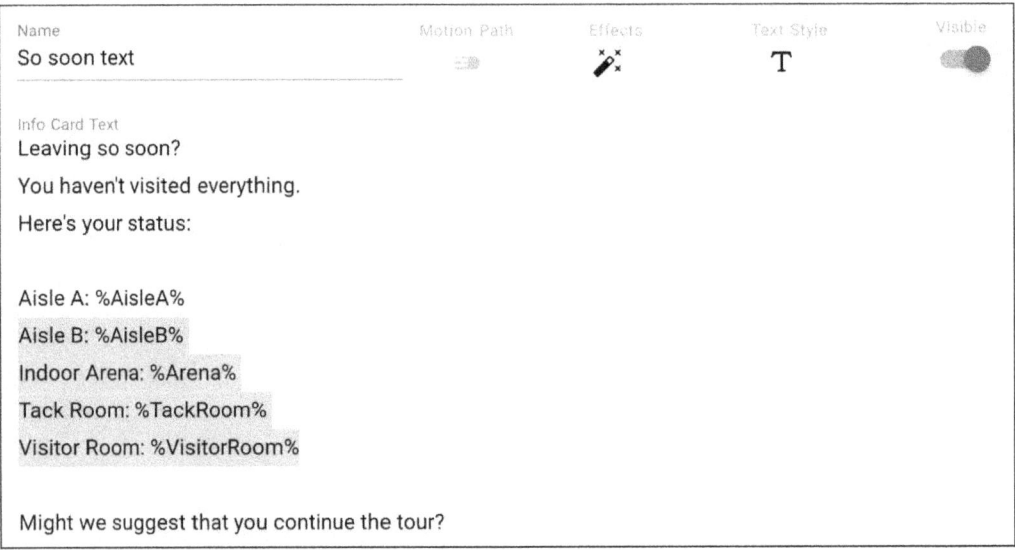

4. Starting with the Barn Entrance scene, preview the project.

5. Move from room to room.

6. At any time, leave the barn through either door.

   If you haven't visited every room, you'll be alerted and any unvisited rooms listed as appropriate.

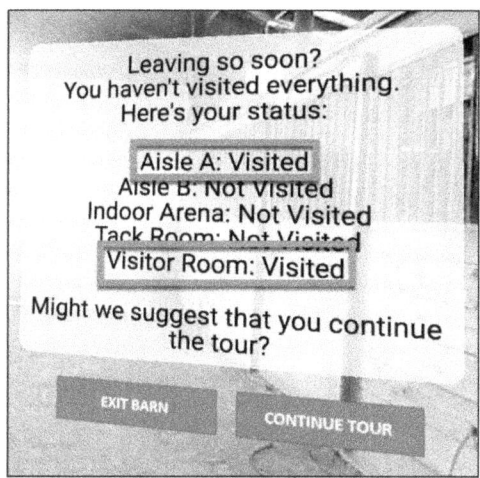

7. Return to Edit mode.

Notes

"Skills and Drills" Learning

Module 6: Publishing

In This Module You Will Learn About:

- Scenario Settings, page 104
- Publishing, page 107

And You Will Learn To:

- Edit Scenario Settings, page 104
- Publish as HTML5, page 108
- Publish as SCORM, page 110

Scenario Settings

Later in this module, you will publish your completed CenarioVR project in multiple outputs including HTML5 and SCORM. But before you reach that endgame, let's finish with a few house-cleaning chores such as the name of the project, the scenario thumbnail, and the preloader.

Scenario Name. The name seems innocent enough, but it's worth a little bit of forethought. The Scenario name will be included in the published package name. In addition, the name appears in the title bar of the learner's web browser.

Scenario Thumbnail. The thumbnail is the miniature image you see when you see your scenarios on the My Scenarios screen. Depending on where your output is hosted, the thumbnail might also be seen by your learners.

Scenario Preloader. The preloader is what is seen by the learner as they wait for the lesson to load in their browser or headset.

Guided Activity 33: Edit Scenario Settings

1. Ensure that you are logged into CenarioVR and on the **My Scenarios** screen.

2. Import the **PublishMe.zip** project from **CVRData > scenarios**.

3. Open the **PublishMe** scenario.

4. Change the Scenario's name.

   ☐ click **Scenario Settings and Publish**

   ☐ click **Scenario Settings**

   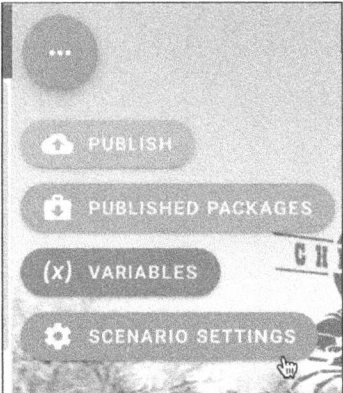

   The Scenario Settings open.

Module 6: Publishing > Scenario Settings > Edit Scenario Settings

☐ change the **Name** to **Your first name Masters CenarioVR**

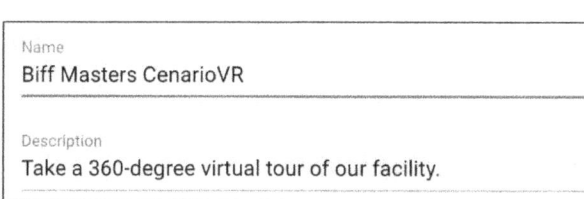

5. Change the Scenario's Thumbnail image.

   ☐ from the **Scenario Thumbnail** area, click **Change**

   The Select New Thumbnail screen opens. From here, you upload an image to use as a thumbnail or use an image from any of the project's scenes.

   ☐ click the **Upload** icon

   ☐ from **CenarioVRData > images and videos**, open **ScenarioThumbnail.jpg**

   The uploaded image replaces the previous scenario thumbnail.

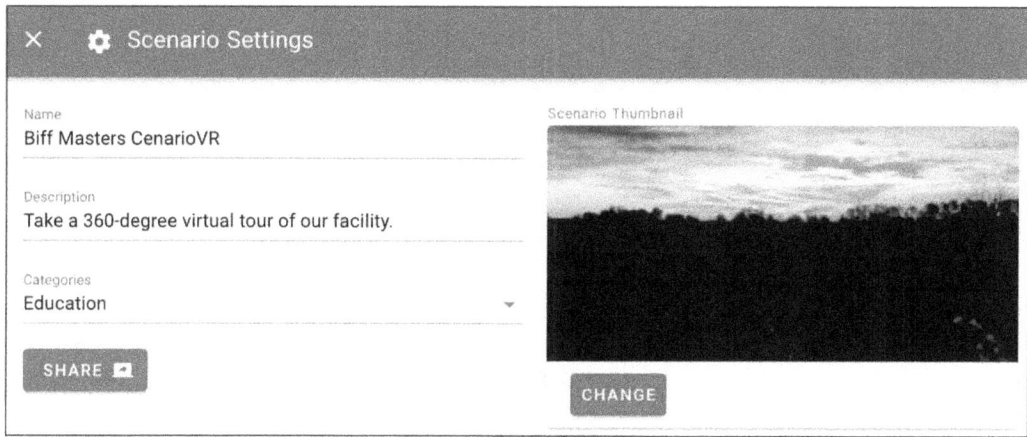

6. Change the Scenario Preloader.

   ☐ from the **Scenario Preload** area, click **Change**

   The Edit Preload Options appear.

   ☐ from the **Preload Options** drop-down menu, choose **Custom**
   ☐ from the bottom of the screen, click **Logo**
   ☐ click the **Upload** icon
   ☐ from **CenarioVRData > images and videos**, open **ChesapeakeStablesLogo.jpg**

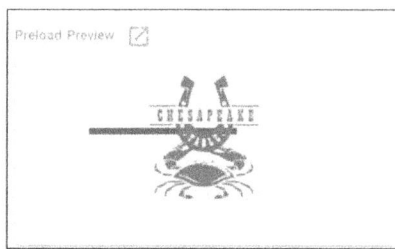

☐ click **Save**

☐ click **Save**

Note: The remaining activities in this book cover publishing. You cannot publish with the CenarioVR trial. If you are using the trial, review the remaining activities, but it's unlikely that you will be able to complete them.

Publishing

Once your project is complete, you're ready to output a version of your course that can be accessed by learners who don't own CenarioVR. This final process is known as publishing. CenarioVR includes several publishing outputs including CenarioVR Live, HTML5, xAPI, cmi5, SCORM 1.2 or 2004. Windows Offline, and Hybrid SCORM.

HTML5: Publishing to HTML5 gives you a zip file containing encapsulated WebXR runtime with your content that you can run on any web server. Use this output type if you are embedding your content within a traditional authoring tool such as **Lectora**, **Articulate Storyline**, or **Adobe Captivate**.

SCORM 1.2 and SCORM 2004: Publishing as SCORM results in a SCORM package that can be uploaded to any SCORM-compliant LMS. The output package includes the manifest, quiz score, and completion status.

CenarioVR Live: This selection publishes to the CenarioVR platform which serves as a sort of LMS. CenarioVR Live includes the ability to utilize the native Apps that come with CenarioVR for many platforms, the use of CenarioVR's Content Delivery Network that enables fast transfer of large video content across the globe, and full xAPI analytics which are built into CenarioVR and provide insight into how your scenarios are being used. Content can be published as either **Private** (it is only visible to specific learners) or **Public** (visible to anyone on the Internet and does not require a login for access).

xAPI: If you are placing your content on an LMS/LRS that is xAPI capable, this is the way to go. This will provide you with all of the same xAPI data that you get when running on CenarioVR, but passed to your LRS. The zip package produced is a fully encapsulated WebVR runtime with an xAPI manifest.

cmi5: This is the newest eLearning standard, and is based on xAPI. If you have a cmi5 compliant LMS, this should be your choice. The zip package produced is a fully encapsulated WebVR runtime with a cmi5 manifest.

Windows Offline: Creates a zip file for Windows 10 or newer. This output does not need to be uploaded to a web server and once unzipped, the content can be used locally.

Hybrid SCORM: Combines the best features of SCORM with the power of the CenarioVR Platform. You can use this standard to upload to any LMS and capture completion data. You can also capture analytics reporting via xAPI using CenarioVR's built-in Learning Records Store, including the ability to create and track custom analytics.

Guided Activity 34: Publish as HTML5

1. Ensure that you are in your "Masters CenarioVR" scenario.

2. Publish as HTML5.

    ☐ click **Scenario Settings and Publish**

    ☐ click **Publish**

    The Publish options appear.

    ☐ from the **Publish Type** drop-down menu, choose **HTML5**

    ☐ if necessary, enable **Scored**

    ☐ change the **Passing Score** to **50**

Recall that your project has a two-question quiz in the Tack Room scene. If learners get one of the questions correct, they'll pass the quiz.

☐ from the upper right of the Publish options, click **Publish**

Once the Publish process is complete, the **Published Packages** screen opens.

☐ click the **Download** icon

The zipped package is downloaded. Typically, the download location is the Downloads folder on your computer.

3. Review the contents of a zipped package.

    ☐ locate the zipped package that you just published and unzip it

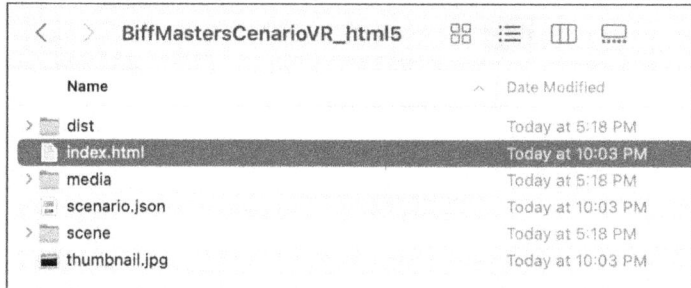

Everything inside the unzipped folder needs to be uploaded to the web server. Once uploaded, anyone clicking a link that opens the index.html page will be able to access the entire published project.

If you'd like to check out a published project, I uploaded my published HTML5 content to my web server. You can interact with the published project here: https://iconlogic.com/elearning/cenariovr/index.html.

CenarioVR: The Essentials (Second Edition)

SCORM

Developed by public- and private-sector organizations, the Shareable Content Object Reference Model (SCORM) is a series of standards that specifies ways to catalog, launch, and track course objects. Courses and management systems that follow the SCORM specifications allow for sharing of courses among federal agencies, colleges, and universities. There are two primary versions of SCORM: version 1.2, released in 1999, and version 2004.

Guided Activity 35: Publish as SCORM

1. Ensure that you are in your "Masters CenarioVR" scenario.

2. Publish as a SCORM package.

   ☐ click **Scenario Settings and Publish** and then click **Publish**

   The Publish options appear.

   ☐ from the **Publish Type** drop-down menu, choose **SCORM 1.2**

   ☐ ensure that **Scored** is enabled and that the **Passing Score** to **50**

   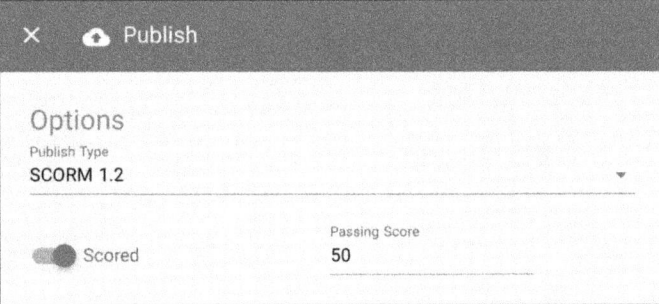

   ☐ from the upper right of the Publish screen, click **Publish**

   Once the Publish process completes, the **Published Packages** screen reopens with both of your published packages.

   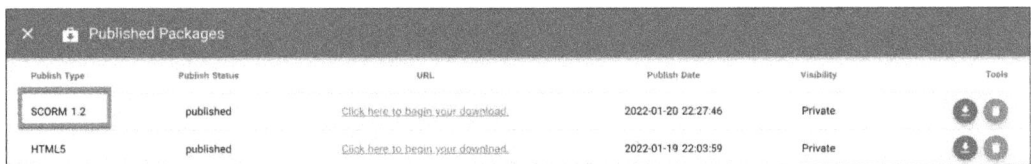

   ☐ click the **Download** icon for the **SCORM 1.2** package

   The zipped package is downloaded, As with the HTML5 zip, the download location is likely the Downloads folder on your computer. The zip would just need to be uploaded to your LMS and you're all set.

   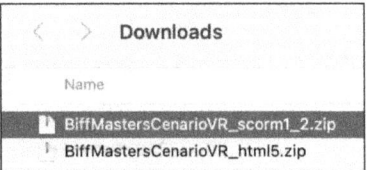

Publishing Confidence Check

1. Publish to **CenarioVR Live**.

   Note: If you leave the Private option enabled, only people who you invite via a URL will have access to the lesson.

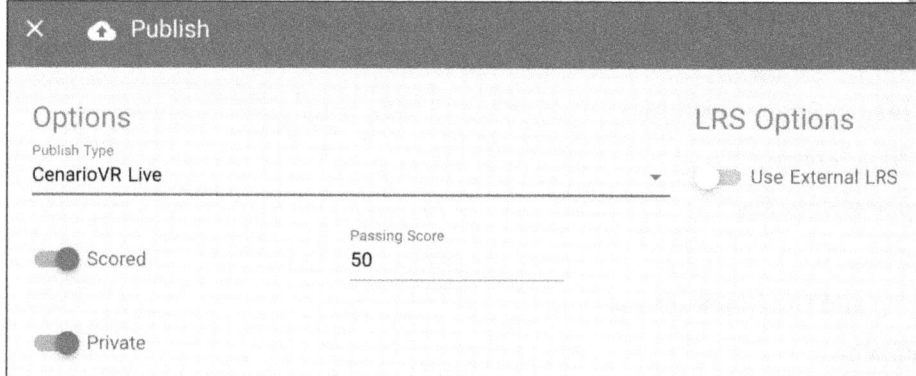

In the Published Packages area, notice that the published content includes a URL link.

2. Right-click the link and copy the link address. You can share the link with a friend or team member and ask them to access your published lesson.
3. Return to the **My Scenarios** screen.

Take a Bow!

Hey, look at that. You have completed this book. Congratulations, you're well on your way to becoming a VR eLearning rock star!

Here are some of the hot skills you've gained as you worked through the past hundred pages or so:

- ❒ Creating Scenarios
- ❒ Adding Scenes
- ❒ Creating Scenes with AI
- ❒ Adding Images
- ❒ Adding Hotspots
- ❒ Adding Audio
- ❒ Drag and Drop Interactions
- ❒ Actions
- ❒ Conditional Actions
- ❒ Quizzes
- ❒ Variables
- ❒ Publishing as HTML5
- ❒ Publishing as SCORM

and...

- ❒ Publishing to CenarioVR Live

I hope you have enjoyed this learning journey. If you need additional help learning or working with CenarioVR, I offer instructor-led CenarioVR training, live online CenarioVR mentoring and support, and complete eLearning development services. You'll find me online at www.iconlogic.com. You can reach me personally via email at ksiegel@iconlogic.com.

Index

A
About the Authors, vi
Actions, 31
Actions, Copying and Pasting, 89
Add a Play audio action to a hotspot, 43
Add Event at current time icon, 75
Add Hotspot, 31
Add Object icon, 31
Add Scene, 14, 15
Add Scene icon, 14, 15
Add to Layer, 64
Add Variable, 97
Adding 3D Images, 37
Adobe Captivate, 107
Adobe Photoshop, 2
AI Wizard, 15
AI Wizard button, 15
Analytics, 107
Animation actions, 77
Articulate Storyline, 107
Asset Requirements, viii
Audio
    MP3, 40
Audio Autoplay, 43
Autoplay, disable, 60, 61

B
Back to Properties button, 28
Backups, 9, 20
Blackmon, John, 2
Book Conventions, vi, vii

C
Camera Positioning, 5
Card Color, 28
CenarioVR, 2
CenarioVR Interface, 8
CenarioVR Live, 107
CenarioVR Live and Mobile, 107
Choose An Action, 31, 34
cmi5, 107
Color opacity, 27
Conditional action, 75
Confidence Checks, vii
Content Delivery Network, 107
Copy Actions, 89
Create New Motion Path, 78
Create Scenario button, 13
Custom Preloader, 105
Custom variables, 97

D
Data Files, download from the Web, viii
Delete a Scenario, 18
Description area, 13
Drag Items, 69
Dragging and dropping, 68
Drop Area, 68, 69
Drop Spot - Single Object, 68, 69

E
Edit mode, 24, 26, 32, 33, 41
Edit Mode Visibility, 87
Edit Scene Properties, 98
eLearning development services, 112
Equirectangular images and videos, 2
Export a Scenario, 20
Export CenarioVR projects, 9

F
Filming with a 360 camera, 4
Font, 27, 28

G
GoProMax, 3
Grid View, 12

H
Hotspot properties, 25
Hotspots, 11, 23
How Software Updates Affect This Book, ix
HTML5, 104, 107
Hybrid SCORM, 107

I
IconLogic, vi
Images and videos, 29
Import a Project, 8
Import Scenario, 9, 22
Info Card options, 27
Info Card, adding, 27, 29, 50, 51, 52
Initial View, setting, 30
Insta360 Nano, 3
Insta360 One X2, 3
Interactive, 68, 69
Interactive Type drop-down menu, 68, 69

J
John Blackmon, 2
JPEG files, 2

L
Layers, create, 64
Learn and retain, 82
Learning can be exhausting, 82
Link To Scene, 33
List View, 12
Login, 8
Logo, 105

M
Media Library, 23, 37
Mentoring, 112
Modify Variable, 98
Modify Variable action, 98
Motion Paths, 78
MPEG Audio Layer III, 40

N
Naming scenes, 17
New scenes, 14

O
Object Actions, 33
On Drop, 70
On Select, 44
On Show Actions, 60, 61
Opacity, 27
Output, 107

P
Pan To, 33
Panning, 33
Passing Score, 108, 110
Paste Actions, 89
Pencil icon, 11
Platform specific, 62
Preload Options, 105
Preloader, 105
Preview Mode, 11
Preview mode, 24, 25, 32, 33, 40
Private, 107
Public, 107
Publish as HTML5, 108
Publish as SCORM, 110
Publish options, 108, 110
Publish to CenarioVR Live, 108
Publish Type, 108, 110
Published Packages, 108, 110
Publishing, 107

Q
Quiz Question, 82
Quiz Question Feedback, 87
Quiz, Choice Text, 85
Quizzes, 82

R
Realism, 15

Remove Event, 78
Remove from layer, 65
Reset, 72
Reset a scene, 96
Roller coaster Effect, 5

S
Scenario Name, 104
Scenario Preloader, 105
Scenario Settings, 16, 97, 104
Scenario Settings and Publish, 104, 108, 110
Scenario Thumbnail, 104
Scenario Thumbnail area, 105
Scenario Thumbnail image, 105
Scenario, Export, 20
Scenarios and Scenes, Manage, 16
Scene Description, 15
Scene Direction, 36
Scene Properties, 17
Scenes, 31
Scored, 108, 110
SCORM, 104, 110
SCORM 1.2/2004, 107
Select Category, AI, 15
Semicircle images, 6

Set Initial, 30
Set Variable Value, 98
Size, 27
Software Requirements, viii
Stitching, 6
Stop Audio action, 44
Switch between scenes, 10

T
Teleporting, 5
Text Style, 28
Thumbnail images, 10
Timed event, 75
Timed event, remove, 78
Timed Events, 75
Training, vi, 112
Transparent, 34
Transparent Hotspots, 34

U
Upload, 9, 22
Upload icon, 31

V
Variables
    Add, 97

Creating, 97
Quiz Results, 92
Reference in an Info Card, 93
Variables and Completion area, 98
Variables, Completion and Automation, 98
Virtual Reality Training, Getting Started, 2
VR cameras, 3
VR users, 62

W
Web Links, 34
WebXR runtime, 107
Windows Offline, 107

X
xAPI, 107

Z
Zipped project, 20

www.ingramcontent.com/pod-product-compliance
Lightning Source LLC
Chambersburg PA
CBHW081840170426
43199CB00017B/2798